FLY

FLY

*Take your BUSINESS to NEW HEIGHTS using the 7
POWERFUL STEPS of **STORY ACCELERATION***

JED BURDICK

For my parents, Allen and Ruth Burdick. Thank you for showing me what love means.

CONTENTS

INTRODUCTION:

All of our consciousness are stories.

Our memories are stories
Our dreams at night are stories
The fiction we read are stories
The movies we watch are stories
The news we hear are stories
The plans we make for tomorrow are stories
In fact, our entire existence is **story**.

And yet, many of us don't recognize the influential power this force has on our lives and the lives of those around us. The raw potential of life's stories is like strong gusts of wind in a sudden storm. We often can't see them coming but, in a blink, the trees around us are bending, random debris go rolling across the land like tumbleweeds, and we run for cover. Quickly shutting the door behind us we hope the creaking house can withstand the wind.

Life is full of unpredictable moments, and they can be terrifying.

But those who learn to embrace the sudden conflict and shape a more powerful story are like the pilot who has his flying machine ready.

He jumps on, cuts the anchor rope, and pedals the contraption with all his might. He's been expecting the storm and the wind that comes with it.

He is ready to fly.

The dance between both writing the story you want to live (action) and leveraging circumstances beyond your control (reaction) is like harnessing the power of the storm.

You can either wait, hide, and hope the house doesn't cave in... or you can ride the wind, sailing higher and higher with every gust the storm throws at you, eventually rising above the storm where the air is steady and calm.

Up there you can see miles, and nothing stands in your way.

Let me tell you about a storm that almost broke me.

"Are we rich?"

Each of my five sons have asked me the same question in a quiet moment, usually around age 7, and often when spending some special one on one time together. The conversation usually goes like this:

"Dad... Are we rich?"

"Yes! We're rich in love! And we have the freedom to continuously learn and enjoy our life together!"

"I mean are we rich with money?"

"Yes... look at all the opportunities and experiences (and yes, things) we're able to have because we have the financial ability... but that's only a part of what gives our life it's richness."

I remember this conversation coming up again with one of my older sons sometime during the summer of 2011. At the time, I didn't feel like talking.

I was incredibly stressed. I was in the middle of another big fight with my wife. At that time, our fights were constant and would bring us to tears almost every day. On this particular day, my bank account was overdrawn, we had almost no food in the cabinets, we hadn't paid our mortgage in more than a year, the sheriff had served us a notice that our home had a date set for public auction. The utility company had warned us they would shut off the power one month prior; we had no credit. I had no current work, no clients, and zero prospects. I couldn't use my normal excuse, "I'm waiting for checks, honey."

As I sat in my garage office with my 9-year-old son, I couldn't stop hearing Bethany's sobbing voice pleading with me, echoing through my head: "Please get a job... it's time to get a job, the business isn't working! We have 5 kids to feed... how am I going to feed them?"

Then from next to me my son asks, "Are we rich"?

I didn't want to answer. I felt very, *very* poor. I remembered Robert Kiosaki's words from *Rich Dad Poor Dad*.

"Yes, we're rich," I answered, "because even when we're broke, we can create new opportunities."

That reminder shot some energy into me. I swiveled back to my computer screen and started scrolling through old emails believing there must be an old prospect, some missed opportunity in there, someone I could call!

My son continued: "Yeah but do we have money like most people?" As much as we tried to hide it from the kids, they inevitably picked up on financial struggles. Kids are smart. I tried to stay ahead of him.

"Well... we actually do have more money than most people."

"We do?"

"Yes. When God looks down on this earth, most of the people he sees only eat rice every day, don't have even one car, don't have easy access to health care, and live in a tiny little place... and toughest part is, most everyone else around them is in the same boat so they have very little opportunity to change their situation."

"They must be so sad."

I thought about that. "Well, I'm sure it's just like here. Some are sad, some are happy, and everyone is some combination of both sad and happy from time to time." I felt better. I knew what I was saying was true! We're going to be okay, I thought, everything is going to be okay. We're going to make it if I can just find a prospect in these old emails. I'll show her, I'll make her proud again, this will be a story which will make us stronger someday when this is all behind me-

CLICK. My screen died. No lights, no sounds. No electricity.

My heart jumped into my throat as I sprang to the door. I saw the power company truck driving off.

"NO!" I shouted. My son went inside.

I called the utility and gave them a postdated check over the phone. I knew it would bounce but maybe it would get the electric on. They assured me the "payment" would restore the power... tomorrow. I pleaded. "I'm sorry sir... there's nothing I can do today." I sat in the dark for a while not wanting to go into the house to face the family.

When I finally went into the house, no angry words were shouted. My wife's silence was deafening. She wasn't punishing me; she's not like that. There was simply nothing left to say. It was still early evening, but she went to bed, exhausted.

I fumbled through the dark house toward the kids' bedrooms. The youngest two were already asleep. The older three shared a room and were still lying awake. I could tell they were feeling the weight of their parents' stress. My heart hurt. I hadn't provided... my main job. *Am I failing as a father?* I certainly felt worthless as a husband. I had to somehow shake off the pain and fear and salvage this moment with my boys.

I pulled the mattresses off their bed and laid them out on the floor. "We're camping tonight!" I blurted with faux excitement.

They eagerly grabbed their blankets and we all stretched out on the floor with flashlights.

After we played, joked, wrestled, and then finally settled, we laid quietly, clicking the flashlights off. I was about to go back to my room when I felt my oldest two were still awake.

"Life has ups and downs," I said in the darkness. "We can't enjoy the ups if we don't experience the downs. When you go to school and look around at all your friends tomorrow you might be tempted to think, 'Do they lose their electricity?' And maybe they never will, maybe they won't try to build a business either. Or maybe there is a way to build a business without this many challenges. But that's all it is, challenges, and life has challenges either way. Tomorrow the power will be back on, and we will keep learning how to overcome more challenges, right?"

"Right," two little voices echoed back from the darkness.

Ups & Downs

If you think about it, almost everything in life is made of wave cycles. Light, sound, radio, electrons, sleep, seasons, weather, DNA, market trends, style trends, bowel movements, brainwaves, labor pains, heartbeats. Even quantum mechanics, the underlying foundation of all physics is actually... a wave.

It should be no surprise that **story** is also a wave, constant change in a repeating pattern. It goes up and comes down and back up again while traveling in a particular direction. How can we enjoy the up if we don't experience the down?

If you study the main characters of your favorite TV shows you'll see they are on a never-ending cycle of being emotionally ripped apart, healing, growing, then it all repeats but with new details.

If you're married or have a long-time partner you understand there are seasons where you are closer and further apart. Where the partnership is more effective and less effective, where there is more romance and then less.

But isn't it interesting that when we're in a difficult season we usually don't say "This is a tough season"? Usually we say something like, "This isn't working" or "I'm done with this", or "You've changed".

We're incredibly emotional beings. In fact, scientists estimate 90% of our decisions are made from the emotional areas of the brain.[1] When we're low, our feelings lean toward thoughts of self-doubt, bridge burning, chapter ending, always and forever types of phrasing.

We don't intuitively recognize that the wave we are caught in is, in fact, a force that can be leveraged and take us to new places. It's a cycle that moves us forward just like the waves that brought us to where we are today.

Prison Break - Part 2 (The Sequel)

I'll tell you the story of *Prison Break: Part 1* near the end of this book, but for now, let's continue where we left off.

The day after my electricity was cut, I did some soul searching. I had real problems that needed real answers. I remembered an acquaintance, a fellow entrepreneur who had mentioned he went through financially tough times. I thought, "He lived to tell about it, maybe I can get some tips from him."

With very little faith, I asked Charbel for a meeting and he invited me to come to his office right away. We had lunch and I humbly shared with him my business challenges and money woes. He listened carefully and asked smart questions. When I had answered, he dove into the details of his story.

We talked for hours. He humbly spelled out the dirty details of his missteps and the hard lessons he learned during the 2008 financial crisis. He told me the raw uncut stories about properties lost, the stress, the fights in *his* marriage, and the scraping change together to buy diapers.

It was exactly what I needed to hear. Suddenly I didn't feel alone; The power of his story was slowly reviving my faith. I felt my strength coming back... and almost as soon as it came, I remembered my reality and felt heavy again. Very heavy.

"I don't think I can do it," I said, referring to pursuing my business. "The needs of my family are too immediate. If it was just me, maybe, but... I have to think about them."

Charbel asked me a wise question, "What will be the faster path to getting paid, hitting the streets, and looking for a job, or hitting the streets and filling your sales pipeline?"

I didn't know the answer. But either way, I knew I would have to sell. Either sell someone on the belief I would be a good hire or sell more of my company services. **I saw that I needed to become a more active character in my story.**

He went on to tell me about the steps he took to increase his effectiveness in sales during times of crisis. He especially focused on some tactics to not look desperate while slogging through seasons of genuine desperation.

I was energized and told him I was ready to get to work. Charbel purchased about a month's worth of my company services then and there. I was floored; he had brought my business back to life.

I almost gave up that day, but the power of his stories helped me push on. I will forever be grateful for this, Charbel. Thank you.

This is where the listener tends to instinctively think "happily ever after" but that isn't real life. I have had many more brushes with financial ruin, and truthfully, so has Charbel! But we recognize that life is a journey, and the journey is filled with stories, an endlessly dynamic cycle of trial and triumph (and tragedy).

Consider for a moment what would have happened if Charbel hadn't told me the stories of his losses, his pain, and the lessons he learned. Critical change would not have happened for me that day and he wouldn't have the benefit of the reminder. But by telling the story, its power compounded and spilled over, becoming available to anyone willing to hear it.

This is the magic of *telling* stories. The more people who hear, the more impact the story has.

Since the time of this story with Charbel, my wife and I have been able to rebuild our marriage, grow a very successful business, and devote more time to our family. We've shared our battle stories with countless couples and entrepreneurs. It's impossible to know how many people they have told and just how far the positive impact has compounded and rippled outward but every once in a while, someone will mention how our story helped them. That's ultimately why this all matters.

Story & Business

Story is not just philosophically important to me. I am in the business of storytelling. Votary Films is the production company I lead. We have the privilege of serving our partners by pouring our creativity into telling their stories in deep and meaningful ways through film and video.

We have found good storytelling to be so effective in marketing, we have started to leverage *story* in other areas of business like building a thriving culture and unstoppable operations.

In our client partnerships, every month we create film and video series such as:

- Deeply engaging customer case study videos (Sales & Marketing)
- Documentary Series about team members solving problems (Culture + Recruiting)
- Engaging Training films teaching standard work techniques (Operations)
- Video Podcasts with the owners & thought leaders (Marketing + Recruiting)

- Team Member "hero highlight" showing an achievement (Culture)
- And many other types of stories

We've helped our partners generate millions in revenue, millions of views, recruit incredible teams and impact society in positive ways.

As much as we love film & video, the real secret behind Votary's success is not the motion picture, but rather the craft of good storytelling. And while our team is made up of *amazing* storytellers, our films/stories are effective because we lean into the **7 Steps of Story Acceleration**, both instinctively and intentionally.

Oftentimes, a client wants to jump right to telling the world about their service or product, instead of taking a moment to uncover the deeper story: What led them to imagine this product/service? What did they want to achieve? What action did they take to develop the product/service? What conflicts did they encounter on the way? How did it change them into what they are today? Using this Story Acceleration process, we can uncover a much more meaningful and compelling story.

It took us a long time to lean into the power of storytelling inside our own business. If you own a service business, you can probably relate. It's funny how easily we can develop and execute a strong plan for our clients but don't instinctively practice what we preach! Not too long ago I got really tired of citing the classic "Cobbler's kids have no shoes" saying and we started taking steps to leverage the power of our own stories at Votary.

Sure enough, with every step, we've **accelerated** holistically.

This book is written to help you strengthen your personal story so as to accelerate strong growth in your own life *and* consequently in your organization. I'm also writing this to reinforce these principles in me, and it will consequently be an accelerator in my life and in the lives of our team at Votary!

This book is not a practical guide for where and how to use magic videos for company growth. As I said, the videos are worthless unless the stories are meaningful.

Meaningful stories are all about the change we experience through the cycle of, action, conflict, and lessons learned.

Meaningful change starts with us as leaders. Our stories will never be impactful if we try to fake it. We have to go through the pain of learning these steps firsthand as the main character in our own story in order to know how to leverage it into our organizations.

This book focuses on the individual's journey of growth. By focusing on improving your personal story, you will inevitably improve the story of your organization!

As we dive into the individual 7 Steps of Story Acceleration, imagine yourself as the main character in an epic story. A story where the external battle is business, but it is a battle that can only be won with psychological and emotional improvements. Becoming a hero in your story will take patience and persistence but when you lean into the 7 steps of Story Acceleration with honesty and perseverance, you will take to the sky.

Let's go.

WHAT IS STORY ACCELERATION?

Story exists to help us make sense of everything. It's designed to be a tool to guide us and ultimately advance the human race.

But story is *only* an accelerator by nature, whether in a positive or negative direction.

If my friend tells me a story about a product or service she loves, I will most likely check it out. If she tells me a story about a movie that gave her nightmares... I will most likely avoid it.

If I fabricate lies about someone behind their back (gossip), we both will be accelerated into negative situations. But if I tell the truth (out of love), everyone will ultimately accelerate in a positive direction.

The more compelling the story, the more influence it will have. The more truthful the story, the more long lasting the influence.

The power cycle of a story essentially has two halves: the creation, the **writing**, of the story and then **telling** the story. The full power of a story is only realized when it is told. Many stories never reach their full potential because they are weak in the creation phase, or they are told ineffectively (or not told at all).

The framework we call **Story Acceleration** *increases* effective growth while *decreasing* the time it takes to achieve said growth. Story acceleration allows you to grow stronger (and achieve more of your dreams) in a shorter period of time

In short, it is the process of creating (living) better stories, and then telling them more effectively in order to **positively influence** ourselves and others to make meaningful progress more quickly.

Let's take a look at the flywheel. We use a circle to visualize this framework because stories tend to repeat themselves in some way or another.

STORY ACCELERATION FLYWHEEL

We start in the center of the graphic with **achievement**. A story always centers around an achievement. We all have things we want to achieve. It's the nucleus of a story.

While visualizing the story for what it could be (what we might achieve), we then move to **action**. This is where we put in the work.

When we take action, we inevitably encounter **conflict** and usually many types of conflict which tempt us toward fight or flight.

Conflict provides us with the opportunity to make principled choices based on our character, and consequently further *forms* our **character**: who we are, what motivates us, how we respond in various situations.

As we finish the first phase of writing (living) the story, we move to the second part on the flywheel where we **reflect** on what we have achieved, what we have learned.

By reflecting and beginning the "telling" phase with a focus on **authenticity**, we are essentially saying "Let's be real" and "What could we have done better?" Authenticity frames our thinking around truthful discovery and accurate representation which ultimately guards and protects the power of the story.

This allows us to uncover the true **moral** to the story. The answer to the "**why**" question.

Finally, how we will apply the lessons learned determines how we will effectively **advance.** This includes answering practical questions regarding how to tell the story such as:

1. Who needs to hear this?
2. What format / style (video, written, in person)?
3. When will it be told?
4. Where will it be told?

As our assessments become more accurate, and we intentionally make improvements in both the story creation and the telling, we are *adding energy* to the feedback loop and thus we accelerate our effective progress!

But if we are not intentional about every step in the cycle, we simply spin our wheels, failing to gain traction, or worse, we accelerate in a negative direction.

Our daily story potential is like breathing. All of us are breathing every day, usually without giving it any thought. But by intentionally breathing deeply, in through the nose, out through the mouth, especially in moments of conflict, our heart rate slows, we think more clearly, we feel more deeply, and our daily life improves.

The key is intentionality.

The Compounding Effect

Before we get into the breakdown of each Story Acceleration Step, I really want you to understand what's at stake here with the story you're writing every day, week, month, and year.

We tend to naturally picture growth and loss as a linear progression, but it rarely is! It's almost always logarithmic, exponential, or a combination of both.

As it relates specifically to growth, author Scott Young did a wonderful job explaining these two types of curves.

Young explains that while logarithmic growth curves grow quickly at first, the results, the gains, decrease over time. They become, in fact, more difficult to maintain.

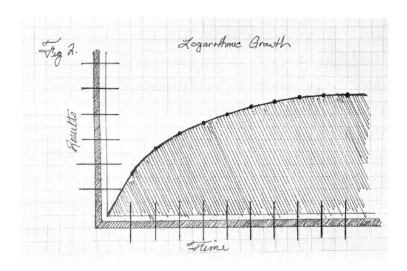

Some examples that Young lists include fitness and strength training; literacy; language proficiency; ability to lose weight; and musical skills, to name just a few.

Exponential growth curves, on the other hand, grow very slowly at first. Then, as time goes one, the results increase rapidly and become easier to maintain!

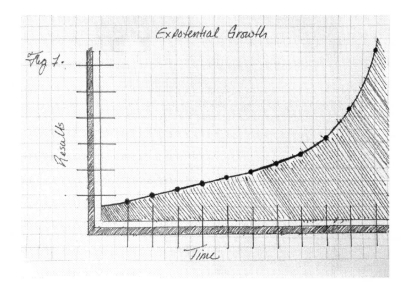

In our everyday life, we see exponential growth in areas like investments and wealth; email subscribers and website traffic; entrepreneurship and business growth; and social media followers.

Neither type of growth is inherently good or bad. However, both types of growth carry very different emotional qualities.

Logarithmic growth curves can be frustrating after the initial spike and make us hungry for increase or breakthrough. When we experience exponential growth, on the other hand, we're often bored for a long time, but then become very excited once we realize we're speeding up. The trap is to see the acceleration as the "new normal" and accept a false sense of security.

The reason for the exponential movement, either up or down, can be found in the impact of the stories that are written, understood, and told prior and during the growth.

Remember what Story Acceleration is: the **writing** and **telling** of stories which increase in value with every chapter. We're writing and telling these stories to both ourselves (what we believe is reinforced by what we experience), and to others (authentic marketing, recruiting, brand awareness, creating a movement, etc.).

Writing and telling epic stories can be defined another way: create immense value, and confidently and authentically show/offer this value.

When we create immense value, it's easier to show and tell this story because people want to see it, hear it, feel it... and ultimately, *share it.*

This is why Story Acceleration (when leveraged properly) compounds your growth. It naturally pulls upward into an exponential curve. The trick is to be patiently persistent. Just like we see with compound interest building our money, it often takes longer than we'd like to learn and apply the lessons from our stories and to experience the acceleration.

Conflict in our stories creates resistance to the growth curve. While we are fighting these battles, time can temporarily outpace the growth. But during this time, intentionally leaning into Story Acceleration allows us to grow the muscle needed for the next upward push.

If we don't fight the battle, however, if we don't learn the proper lessons and adapt and or reinvent, we will plateau and start dying inside. This can happen quickly if we (and those around us) believe our story to be turning irredeemably tragic.

We often see this in the life of a drug user. First, they lose their control over drug usage. Then they lose their job, their family, their positions, their freedom or even their life *if* they don't interrupt the sharp downward curve and fight their way back using the lessons they have learned to gain some assemblance of hope.

It's very hard for a person in this situation to write a new story once they start believing a comeback story is not possible or probable.

Conversely, achievers, the rising stars often go from the dull daily grind of having only few opportunities to having more opportunities than they can handle in a short period of time. This is because Story Acceleration quietly and slowly compounded while they were faithfully grinding away at building a better product or service, building a better team, creating more value for everyone around them. They were patiently writing a better story and gaining the wisdom needed to sustain the compound growth when it tips.

What I'm staying is this: grind on faithfully and lean into the timeless principles for writing a bigger, better story. If you do, *you will accelerate your effective growth rate.*

Here are some of the common experiences leaders enjoy when applying these principles:

- Ever increasing rate of inbound opportunities
- More relationships
- Deeper and more meaningful relationships
- More effective leveraging of time
- More profit
- Shorter recovery times (from setbacks)

Remember the wave of life? It will always go up and down, but by leaning into the positive principles of Story Acceleration *the wave doesn't come back down as far.* This is because the lessons learned are applied, the growth wave consolidates, builds energy, and then shoots higher in the next pass.

How epic of a life story will you write? The answer you give will have the most effect on how much value you add to the world, and how long after you're gone your story is told.

As we journey through these principles, keep in mind that some blend into one another or have similar characteristics. Some may sound obvious and "simple" at first, maybe even familiar, but ideas are usually easy, and application is not. Do yourself, your family, your friends, and your team a favor, focus on applying these ideas rather than writing them off.

Here are the 7 Steps of Story Acceleration.

Part One:

Write The Story

STEP ONE: VISUALIZE ACHIEVEMENT

My palms were sweating, and I almost never sweat. I stared at the phone, trying to plan out the call I had to make. "This could go terribly wrong" I kept thinking. In fact, it was hard to imagine it possibly going well. The story I'm about to tell you will sound like a tale from the 1800s but in fact the year was 1999. I was about to call up a grown man and ask him to grab a pizza so we could chat about something important.

I had shaken Billy's hand once, so I knew he was about 20 years my senior, outweighed me by about 150lbs, had a full beard, and about a million stories tattooed in his eyes. A sense of humor? I didn't know if he had one. What I did know was he had very strong traditional beliefs, and a 17-year-old daughter who was about the prettiest and most interesting girl I had ever laid eyes on.

"Hello?" he answers on the other end of the phone line. I'm pacing now. I manage to clear my 20-year-old throat and muster my best "man" voice.

"Hi Billy, this Jed Burdick. This may sound like a strange request, but I'm wondering if you'd meet me out for a pizza and a chat tomorrow?"

Crickets. More crickets. I feel like I should speak just to break this god-awful silence.

"Okay," he finally pushes out through what I swear sounds like clenched teeth.

I hang up feeling like I just chugged a bowl of soup made of elation and dread. I wasn't sure if I should laugh or throw up.

Before I tell you what happens next, we first have to go backward two months and watch the prequel.

Sobbing on the living room floor of my apartment, I was at the end of the darkest chapter of my life. I felt intensely alone, wrestling with the deepest existential questions: *Why am I here? What am I worth?*

I hadn't been making much progress at work, or in music, or in my writing, I had just come out of a pointless relationship with a girl, and my grandfather (who was a huge influence in my life) had just died unexpectedly.

I laid there thinking about his funeral. Thousands of people came to pay respects, cars lined up for what seemed like miles. I knew what he meant to me, but I had no idea the profound impact this man's life had on so many.

It forced me to look hard at my own life. I won't bore you with all the details, but the short story is that I had wasted most of the year leading up to this moment with selfish living, which slowly, imperceptibly eroded my sense of purpose. I wasn't suicidal, but my loneliness was almost crippling. I wondered the point of achieving anything in this life if I didn't have someone to share it with.

I wanted to share a deep, meaningful, and permanent love with someone. In my gut, I knew that if I could solve this loneliness problem, I would have the energy and motivation to achieve everything else. But finding the right person, that highly compatible someone who would adore the real me, seemed impossible.

As I prayed in the dark, the conversion went something like this:

"God, if you created me then you know me better than I know myself. Can you please connect me with the right person for me?"

Then from somewhere deep inside, I heard a quiet voice say two words:

"Don't worry."

Two weeks later I met Bethany while randomly visiting my parents on their farm about 90 minutes from where I lived. Her family had just bought land nearby and my parents had invited them for dinner.

I couldn't take my eyes off her. It wasn't just her beauty. There was a depth about her. I found out her mother had died one year earlier, and she had to grow up quickly taking on the responsibility of her 5 young siblings. When she looked up and our eyes met, some kind of information was transmitted between us. While I couldn't decipher the information, I knew I felt a depth and energy that's hard to explain.

That night when they left, I said to my mother. "I think I'm going to marry that girl."

As I write this, I imagine it sounds unbelievable or even cheesy. Like bad fiction. But fact is stranger than fiction, they say.

Over the eight weeks that followed, Bethany's family visited my family a lot more. They went to the same church, and I came down every weekend to get as much time around her as I possibly could. Always in a group.

I became more attracted to her each day. She was a hard worker, she didn't gossip, she loved kids... and I could feel her admiration when she looked at me.

But there was a problem. She was 17 and I was 20. How could it possibly work? I imagined it would take years before she would be willing to marry, or for her father to even approve! But I knew she was worth it, so I set my mind to the mission. First, I needed to be patient. I settled myself into the "long haul" mentality. Next, I needed her father to be on board.

Pizza

After we ordered, Billy set his menu down, looked up and calmly said:

"What would you like to talk about?"

This was suddenly way more difficult than I imagined it would be. I stammered and stuttered, but finally got it out.

"I really like your daughter," I said. "I think I might even love her, although I haven't told her that yet... we've only spent time in groups. First, I want you to know my intention. I don't want a cheap relationship; I'm looking for a wife. I know it will take time, but I want to ask your permission to build a relationship with her."

My future father-in-law blinked once or twice before speaking.

"What exactly does 'building a relationship' with her mean to you?"

"I want to call her, and write her, and take her on dates."

He chewed his celery for minute looking up at me once or twice and then said:

"You can call her, you can write her; but you cannot take her on dates."

I processed this.

"But we can hang out in groups?" I asked.

He nodded.

"Deal," I said awkwardly, as if I had bought a horse from the man. I barely stopped myself from initiating a handshake. I felt something big was achieved. And in truth, something was. Billy shifted the conversation to asking all about me. At the time it felt like he was getting to know a new friend but as I write this, I am now roughly the same age he was then, *and* I now have a daughter... he was gathering intel about the enemy.

The next day Bethany and I talked about our feelings for each other for the first time.

Two weeks later, she turned 18 and I gave her a diamond necklace. After all, he didn't say I couldn't give her any gifts. He quickly asked *me* to meet him for pizza. After making it abundantly clear to me that things needed to go excruciatingly slow with "no dating", I agreed, and the conversation turned to other things again.

And that's how it went for 6 months. Instead of "dating" Bethany, I went to pizza with Billy every week. It turned out we loved the same music and movies. We also both enjoyed carpentry and studying ancient bible history.

If I came to his farm and helped him, say, stack wood, or jack up a corner of the barn to repair the foundation... I could also see Bethany. She and I fell madly in love, and truthfully, Billy and I became good friends too.

During the 6 months of weekly pizza "dates", I asked Billy if I could marry his daughter 3 separate times. The third time I asked, he countered with:

"I'm going to Worcester this weekend and I could use some company. Let's you and I take a road trip and I'll give you my answer at the end of the weekend." Was this a test? Take a trip? Why? Is he going to kill me and hide evidence? I was confused, but I went for it.

About 45 minutes into our "road trip" to Massachusetts, Billy told me, with a twinkle in his eye, he'd love for me to join the family and that he'd give his support and blessing for us to get married whenever we chose to.

When we got back, I took Bethany on our very first "alone" date and asked her to marry me. (She said yes).

And so, a little more than 8 months after God introduced me to the love of my life, we said "I do" there on my parent's farm where we met. We've been married for 20 years. In those 20 years, we've had 5 sons and adopted a daughter. We still surprise each other, make each other laugh, lift each other up, and stubbornly fight for the best relationship we can possibly have.

No matter what else I accomplish in my life, marrying Bethany will always be my biggest achievement because sharing everything with her (and our children) gives actual meaning to my life, and I thank God for this almost every day.

My Greatest Achievement

As proud as I am about our beginnings, I don't tell this story to brag. I tell the story because it still surprises me. I still shake my head thinking back on how unique it is compared to most couples' origin stories.

Somehow this amazing girl (and her dad) came to like me, an average looking, Toyota Corolla driving, trench coat wearing, music and story writing geek, who had way too little money, and perhaps way too much naive faith.

I don't look back and think, "Wow, I really had it figured out..."

Instead, I marvel at how little understanding I possessed. I was no chess master. I had no special strategy or proven tactics to employ. The only thing I had was a deep desire in my heart to someday have a love that was real. I wanted a strong relationship, and I was willing to work at it as long as it would take.

I had a vision, and I committed to work at it every day. It's as simple as that. I didn't know the obstacles or the timeline. In a way, that didn't matter.

No matter what else I accomplish, I consider developing a relationship with the love of my life and marrying my wonderful partner, Bethany, the greatest achievement of my lifetime.

Take a moment to think about your own history. Can you think of one personal achievement you are proud of? I'm willing to bet you can, and I am also willing to bet that achievement took quite a while, maybe even years.

It's probably not an achievement you arrived at accidentally. You had to work at it. Let's face it, the short-term future is easy to see and feel. We make plans to go to dinner on Wednesday night and we usually do. We plan to go on vacation in February, and we usually do.

But planning a long-term achievement somehow feels delusional and even irresponsible. We tend to assume it won't happen, as if there are too many unknown variables.

This is because we operate mostly from emotion daily. The brain has a hard time recalling enough detail from our historic memories to feel the proper emotion on command. We see this at play when we stumble upon old photos of the family. Prior to looking at a photo, it's very difficult to "remember" details about our child at three years old. But the moment we see that cute little face from back then, we are flooded with emotion.

"Oh my gosh, look how little he was," we say.

In this regard, we don't naturally feel the value of our past stories (achievements) but we must!

People who have discovered the magic of journaling every day can attest to how powerful it is to read old entries and see how much has been achieved since the time of the entry. It can also be enlightening to see what we "thought" we would have achieved by now but haven't. It begs the question:

1. Was it a worthy goal?
2. Did our belief steadily or abruptly wane (if yes, then why?)
3. Did we simply assume too short a timeline?

The truth is, we don't know how long it will take to achieve a specific goal. The trick is to bring the long-term goals into the present daily cycle of intention and reflection.

Every morning Ben Franklin famously asked himself, "What good shall I do today?" and then in the evening he asked himself, "What good did I do today?" He wasn't randomly choosing the day's activities. He was intentionally planning *how* to achieve the best possible outcome for that day as it related to the long-term goal.

He intentionally pre-visualized optimization, then acted, then reflected, continually seeking the accurate moral to the day's story.

Dreaming vs. Planning

I'm a dreamer. It's just the way I'm wired. It's never been difficult for me to slip into rich detailed fantasies like opening offices all around the world... which of course will require that I buy an apartment in SoHo, a cliff house over Laguna Beach, and a luxury submarine docked in Monaco.

The only real problem is, I need to find a personal chef who is *also* a trained massage therapist, because there really aren't enough seats on my Gulfstream G700 if I go with the triple size Master Suite plus a hot tub option... which is a no brainer.

Ha. No seriously, the only real problem is how will I *not* gain 300lbs when eating at a different Michelin 3-star restaurant every other night (not every night, that's ridiculous). Oh, I think I figured it out: my chef/massage therapist will also be my *personal trainer*, who is also a jiu jitsu trained bodyguard! (Business idea?)

I'm smirking because that fantasy joke went on way too long and came to me a little too easily.

Before you judge me too harshly, a few of my real dreams are:

- use the power of story to match orphans with families
- produce amazing original series about important things like... history
- help as many people out of poverty as I possibly can

- teach carpentry to my future grandchildren.
- And yes, have a luxury submarine

If you're like me, the problem has been too much dreaming, which can lead to "business idea of the month" which leads precisely... *nowhere.*

It's much more difficult to reverse engineer the steps it will take to achieve big long-term accomplishments and work at them patiently and persistently, every day.

We must be keenly aware of our natural tendency to slip into autopilot and forget what we are going after.

Epic achievements require conviction: the deep belief that when we set worthy goals, and intentionally optimize each day, a positive outcome is inevitable!

Long term goals should be so big and so sacred that we are willing to tell everyone about them, often. Because we *know* it's our destiny. There is no reason to be embarrassed or fearful of what it would look like if we don't make it. Yes, we will have to adapt as we go, but we need to be very careful not to change plans just because the work gets difficult.

For me, dreaming helps create energy and motivation, but in order to avoid escaping into "dreamer" mode too often, a helpful hack is to intentionally schedule dreaming time, and only allow extended dreaming in the allotted time slot.

It's also very helpful to write all the "great ideas" which come during dreaming time, and then put them on the shelf for later or never. This exercise tends to foster creative thinking over time. Our subconscious often remembers the ideas before we do and weaves them back into our main path as opportunities when the time is right. What was once a potential distraction becomes a realized story.

Positive Feedback Loop

I knew in the core of my being that someday Bethany and I would be married. Of course, her beauty was a strong continual motivator, but with every positive pizza date I had with her father, I felt just a little more assurance that we were headed in the right direction!

Don't underestimate the power of a positive feedback cycle. We all need it.

The brain is an amazing computer, constantly being programmed to control our body and the outcome of our efforts. According to Dr Sanjay Gupta1, just by changing your thoughts, you can modulate your heart rate, blood pressure and immune system. If you want to be a high achiever, you must train your brain to think in a way that sets you up for success.

The rewiring of your brain is a result of neuroplasticity, which includes two things: neurogenesis (the growth of new neurons) and synaptogenesis (new connections between neurons). We enhance the growth of those two things through meditation, reflective self-inquiry, mindfulness, asking meaningful questions, and visualization.

The two things I want to focus on again are visualization and reflection. Think of it like a question and an answer. When we visualize, we are telling the brain to perform an outcome. But there is a tension here because the brain wants to know if this is possible before creating a habit. Habits are like shortcuts or hacks the brain uses to achieve the goal with the least amount of effort possible later.

When our brain gets the positive feedback it's looking for, reward centers release dopamine.

You've heard the phrase "Practice makes perfect." Vince Lombardi said, "Perfect practice makes perfect." Perfecting the practice is almost more important than focusing on the outcome.

Of course, we can't be "perfect" in our practice, but his point was to immediately release the mistake, correct it, and attempt to focus only on the right habits. It's easy to think of practice as short repetitive cycles, but longer cycles, like daily or weekly stories, are also practice... The brain is still trying to optimize.

After we achieve, even a moderate level of success, when we celebrate that success by highlighting it in a story, we answer the question with "Yes, here's what was possible" and we train the brain to accept our future visualizations as truth.

I hear you asking, "But what if we don't achieve the visualized goal in the assumed time frame?" Even that has a lesson. We can intentionally *release* the guilt, celebrate the effort and the lesson, and then adjust for the next phase. By intentionally completing the cycle of visualization and reflection with a positive outlook, we are programming the brain to trust our commands.

The key is to always allow a reward with dopamine by celebrating the achievement, the effort, and the lesson. We do this by intentionally highlighting one of them in the story!

Therefore, we must start Story Acceleration with visualizing the larger long-term achievements, and then break the journey down into daily bite size achievements. We write the ending to the story (the best we can), then we work at reinforcing the positive neuroscience by celebrating the achievements within the journey: the morals in each chapter. It's a continual process.

This is why the graphic for *Step One: Visualize Achievement* is at the center of the story Acceleration flywheel. No matter where we are in our current journey around the flywheel, we should always visualize what we want to achieve; that is, the best possible outcome.

The 4 Minute Barrier

Beyond what this does to the characters in the story, it has almost the same impact on those who *hear* the story.

Maybe you've heard about the 4-minute mile. Before 1954, it was thought to be impossible because no one had done it. Journalist John Bryant wrote extensively about runners having chased the goal seriously since at least 1886, and that the challenge involved the most brilliant coaches and gifted athletes in North America, Europe, and Australia. "It had become as much a psychological barrier as a physical one," he wrote regarding the 4-minute mile. "And like an unconquerable mountain, the closer it was approached, the more daunting it seemed."[2]

Then on May 6, 1954, at Oxford University's Iffley Road Track, British athlete Roger Bannister broke the 4-minute mile. Just 46 days after Bannister's feat, John Landy, an Australian runner, broke the barrier again, with a time of 3 minutes 58 seconds. Then, just a year later, three runners broke the four-minute barrier in a single race.

There are many stories like the 4-minute mile. Stories of various pioneers of sport and industry achieving something seemingly impossible, and each time many more are suddenly able to follow suit.

When we humans see what's possible in other's stories, it's much easier to believe and then achieve.

This is why case study stores are so powerful, especially in business. A strong story about a product or service genuinely helping a company achieve meaningful results is usually more powerful than a highly creative commercial spot!

My good friend and fellow storyteller, Isaac Deitz, once wrote: "When I was a kid people told me I could be anything I wanted when I grew up... so I told them I wanted to be a dolphin."

I laughed when I read that.

Of course, life has real boundaries. Can a human turn into a dolphin? Well, at this exact moment scientists are indeed pushing all sorts of genetic boundaries, so who knows. I'm mostly kidding.

The question, "Can we?" in many cases, is easier to answer than the question, "Should we?"

The Moral Compass

As we set our sights on big achievements, we must ask ourselves how it connects to a larger spiritual story and decide what we are not willing to compromise throughout the journey lest we lose our way.

King Solomon in the Bible was said to be the wisest man of his time. The Story goes, after King David passed, his son Solomon became king. He felt the weight of the office, so he started by leading all the people in offering a thousand burnt offerings (sacrificial worship).

That night God appeared to Solomon, perhaps in a dream. God said: "Ask me for whatever you want."

"I want wisdom to know how to best lead my people." Solomon said (I'm paraphrasing).

"And God said to Solomon, because this was in thine heart, and thou hast not asked riches, wealth, or honor, nor the life of thine enemies, neither yet hast asked long life; but hast asked wisdom and knowledge for thyself, that thou mayest judge my people, over whom I have made thee king." - 2 Chronicles 1:11

And God did as he promised. Solomon was granted wisdom and knowledge. During his time as king, he was able to unite the people of Israel, he did massive amounts of city development, created amazing allies and trade partners with other people groups, built countless seemingly impossible buildings such as the Hebrew Temple multiple palaces, and a fleet of ships...

and of course he protected it all from those who would like to steal or destroy Israel's wealth.

But as his power grew, so did his ego, and his relationship with God slowly eroded. There were times when he lost his Moral Compass. Despite all of his earthly achievements, Solomon also suffered through great conflict, mostly from his own selfish choices.

Solomon worked hard, he intentionally achieved great things... accomplishments which are impossibly difficult to achieve by today's standards. Yet, after it all he felt compelled to explain that there is "no new thing under the sun"3 that is capable of giving true meaning to our life.

From a personal perspective, Solomon is lamenting that even if wildly huge accomplishments are achieved in the physical realm, death is waiting for us all- we can't take any of it with us. Conflict and pain are inevitable, and answers to the hard questions of life are not forthcoming.

He finishes the twelve, fairly negative chapters of Ecclesiastes with a simple statement: follow God while living this earthly life, because we will ultimately meet with him and have to account for our choices.

No Regrets

If you don't believe in God, let's frame the guiding compass from the perspective of regrets.

Karl A. Pillemer Ph.D. and his team interviewed more than 1500 people over the age of 65 ask specifically what they wish they did differently. He compiled his research into a book titled *30 Lessons for Living: Tried and True Advice from the Wisest Americans*.4

The top 7 are:

1. Not being careful enough when choosing a life partner
2. Not resolving a family estrangement
3. Putting off saying how you feel
4. Not traveling enough
5. Spending too much time worrying
6. Not being honest
7. Not taking enough career chances

It's not surprising to me that the top 3 regrets (and number 6) are simply impediments for sharing love.

The love we share with others is the most important thing in life. It should be the ultimate achievement.

I have never been to a funeral where people cry passionately about someone's earthly achievements, but I've been to plenty where there isn't a dry eye while talking about the love the person gave to others.

It's very important here to understand there are many ways of giving love, including simply being a great example.

If I sat around with no other intention than to play with my kids for the rest of my days, life would fall out of balance very quickly. No work means no money which means no food for my family, which is not very loving.

It's a loving act to lead by example, to dream big, work hard, learn lessons, celebrate, play hard, and repeat in a healthy rhythm. In fact, guiding others into this rhythm is one of the most loving things we can do. We will never regret leading with love.

Remember the importance of the wave, the repeating rhythm. Too much of any one area and we cannot optimize.

Work too much, miss out on love. Work too little, miss out on love.

The most epic achievers, the people who are talked about with deep admiration, for many generations, maintained an extreme commitment to achieving that which would ultimately promote love.

Historical figures like:
Abraham Lincon
Martin Luther King Jr.
Mother Teresa
Mahatma Gandhi
Nelson Mandella

And even entrepreneurs and teachers in our time: Tony Robbins, Robert Kiyosaki, Simon Sinek and many more. They all have a love for their fellow man. You can feel their desire to help others (love) pouring out when they exercise their gifts.

Just like in any good story, the value is in the journey *and* the destination. The destination is diminished if the journey lacks love. The journey is diminished if the destination lacks love.

The big idea I am trying to drive home in this first section about achievement is: **Aiming high and going big is always the right choice when the net result is more love for more people.**

As we move into the application steps and the next sections, I want to refocus you on your entrepreneurial or intrapreneurial journey. How much have you risked and achieved so far? How much are you willing to risk and achieve going forward from here?

EXERCISE: *History*

Download the STORY ACCELERATION WORKBOOK on votaryfilms.com/fly and follow the instructions under Step 1: HIstory. Use the catalyst questions to stimulate your thinking and get it all out, first into scratch paper or a typed document.

Don't listen to *any* type of internal negativity. Just write your achievements, both big and small, as short paragraphs. Don't spend much time thinking about "what you should have done."

I am intentionally starting you with these exercises so that you can see just how many stories you currently have and will have! Each story you wrote can and should be told carefully, to the right audience, at the right time. Telling these battle stories will accelerate the larger story.

We will build off this template as we move through the action steps so take your time and really get everything out here.

Get to it!

STEP TWO: TAKE ACTION

In his book *Think and Grow Rich,* Napoleon Hill outlines 13 principles for success obtained after interviewing more than 500 Millionaires. Every single one of those 13 principles involves taking *action* either mentally or in the physical.[1]

Deciding to be *active* instead of *passive* is critical to writing our story. This may seem obvious when we're analyzing someone else's story because without action they simply look boring, fearful, or lazy; but what about our own story?

As much as we like to feel safe in the planning phase, the real work is done when we take action. **The more action you take, the more story you are writing**. And consequently, the more fuel you are giving your growth engine.

Take a moment and watch a movie of yourself from the last couple of days. You woke up yesterday and then... It's hard to even remember, right? Okay, how about today? What do your decisions look like? How active or passive are you being? What action steps could you take to really move your story? Could you get them done while maintaining a fun and pleasant spirit? What does the future you think of your daily amount of action and the direction you're heading?

If you haven't distilled your dreams down into worthy goals and actionable steps, it makes sense if you're not yet taking aggressive action. Read this chapter as if your dream goals are written and you're ready to work.

Three Villains

There are only three reasons people don't take massive action toward their goals:

1. Laziness
2. Fear
3. Distraction

All three can be very difficult to shake depending on how deeply our habits are set, but rest assured the power of story can vanquish these ugly villains.

The antidote to laziness is achievement as we've discussed in the former chapter. The dopamine of meeting milestones feels oh so good, it will have us coming back for more... unless of course it's blocked by fear or distraction.

Let's take a closer look at these last two.

Distraction is perhaps more powerful than ever before in history. Our modern way of life embraces perpetual distraction. Even as I am writing this, three people have walked into my office (because my door is open), I checked my phone at least three times, my email twice, I keep changing the music playlist to find a better writing mood.

Just keep writing, Jed.

Multi-tasking is a productivity trap. It looks sexy when the hero, speeding down the highway, explains what's at stake to her passenger, while being chased, while she hacks into the mainframe with her phone in one hand and a gun in the other, steering with her knees! "Get down!" she yells. BLAM-BLAM-BLAM. She fires through the back window.

CRASH. She hits the median. She should have had her eyes forward and hands on the wheel. Too bad. She was amazing.

Single tasking really is a superpower. Once we have our work prioritized, if we want to really make progress to be proud of, we must eliminate all distractions.

Tell everyone when you'll become available again, go to a quiet place, face away from everyone, close your email, no more desktop notifications, and for goodness' sake, turn off your phone.

If your work involves meeting with others, shut yourself away and prepare. Then allow no distractions in the meeting. Going slow with one person at a time, is really going faster in the long run.

Sounds awful, right? At first, it is. We can go through withdrawal similar to coming off other harmful drugs. But over time your brain chemistry resets. Abstaining from the stimulation of distraction allows you to get higher from your micro achievements!

Social media can be one of the most difficult distractions to eliminate. I recommend going off cold turkey and staying off. If your work directly involves social media for marketing, set painful limits on your usage sprints. Without harsh limits we're inevitably hypnotized, lured toward the purple light like a bug flying blissfully into the zapper on the patio.

Planning and research can also be bottomless pits of distraction when we really should be putting in the work.

Why? Because the research and planning are safe! Once we break from cover and start taking action, we move from theory to reality... and reality is scary.

See, under the surface, sometimes undetectable, we are all facing a much bigger villain, the third and most heinous, hideous, and venomous, of the three villains...

Fear. We're afraid of what people will think. We're afraid we're not good enough. We're afraid they will find out we're faking it. We're afraid it won't work out; afraid it will be a waste of time... we're afraid of *pain*.

It's built into us. Some say it's a "self-preservation" mechanism from evolution. Maybe. To me, it feels like a spiritual force working against us. Conversely, deeply creative ideas that seem to come from nowhere, also feel spiritual... seemingly designed by someone else but handed to us.

In his wonderful book *The War of Art*, Stephen Pressfield does a superb job describing the invisible forces that seem to work both for us and against us.

He writes, "If you were meant to cure cancer or write a symphony or crack cold fusion and you don't do it, you not only hurt yourself, even destroy yourself; You hurt your children. You hurt me."2

The work of a creative, Pressfield argues, is not a selfish or attention-seeking act. Instead, it's a necessary gift to the world.

Pressfield continues, stating that the resistance we experience when we begin to do that work is actually fear. The resistance increases with the fear. The fear is, in fact, a sign that the work we are about to set out to do is so important and necessary to the growth of our soul. "If it meant nothing to us," he states, "there'd be no Resistance."3

Even when we're not conscious of the fear, it's looming in the background offering us distractions to keep us from taking action and breaking from cover.

Maybe you feel a lack of progress in your story. Maybe you're frustrated by distractions and self-destructive forces that seem to rally when you attempt to make progress.

The key to breaking through is this: bring the fear out of the hidden shadows of our heart and into the light where it can be disinfected with truth... then begin to take action.

Smarter *AND* Harder

In recent years, hustle has been fetishized.

Working hard and learning perseverance is very important. However, the idea that hustle is all you need for success can lead to a frustrating lack of progress if we're not "hustling" on the most effective activity. Thinking long term and applying it to short term steps prevents meaningless hustle.

Don't get me wrong, I think regular sprints are incredibly valuable. We've all had that final push when a deadline is looming or when you're about to go on vacation and certain things just have to get done. It's surprising how much we can achieve, or how creative we can be when we have to.

It's better to work harder *and* smarter. We can easily work ourselves into a frenzy and get almost nowhere if we don't work smart; that is, if we don't choose the right tasks.

Working smarter *and* harder is all about thinking ahead, anticipating problems before they arise, then prioritizing the tasks that are most important, and then digging in like your life depends on it.

Our main character in a strong story needs to think both long term and short term. Long term is legacy, and short-term choices add up and become meaningful change making the legacy a reality.

But how do we ensure we're working smarter? The short answer is **teamwork**.

Teamwork & Accountability

I just wanted to get moving. I was itching with anticipation.
We had taken too long to plan this journey and I didn't want to lose motivation.

"There's gold in that jungle!" I yell to the group.
"I can smell it! Who's with me?" I let out a whoop.

A few excited cheers echo back from the group.
And then one person says, "We've almost finished
prepping, not long before we're done…"

"We were ready a while ago," I say as I start,
hacking into the jungle with a machete called art.

I swing wildly and march north with tunnel vision.
The group follows at a safe distance, while I proudly
make the decisions.

I sprint forward finding the natural paths though the
terrain.
But it's getting harder to see as a cloud settles and
starts to rain.

The group tries to keep up, a few fall behind.
Nothing to worry about, they'll catch up, I decide.

I can hear the foreman yell something about "the
rest."
"The rest will catch up to us," I holler back, my eyes
darting from one obstacle to the next.

I slice the vines down, until a sudden sound:
CRACK! My blade bounces off a rock in the ground.

I look up; there is a whole wall of stone I seem to
have found.
No worries, I think, I am sure we can get around.

The vines are a little thicker now. It's time to sharpen
the blade.
"Bring me the sharpener!" I yell. "And a spade!"

I'm answered by Silence; I turn and glare backward
with disdain.
But no one is there, only the sound of the rain.

"Great," I mutter. Cowards and weaklings.
well, lead by example, I think as I begin swinging.

Sometimes you just need to muscle through.
I take my frustration out on the brush laced with
dew.

WHAM. I go down. A root has my foot.

Damn. I see a blood trickle down my leg; the blade
nicked me good.

I need a bandage from our kit so reluctantly, I double
back.

Around the bend I find the whole team sitting on the
path.
"See, the rest caught up," I quip, trying to swallow
my wrath.

"I said, 'they need a rest', a water break," my second
in command says bluntly, handing me a canteen.
"You need one too, or you'll run out of steam."

"It seems a little early for a rest break," I say,
but the water looks refreshing, I drink it anyway.

"The group had a great idea," he goes on. "They stood
on each other's shoulders and climbed to the top of
that palm."
He points to a big tree and continues with glee.

"Now that we are on high ground, they saw a stream to the west-"

"But we're going north!" I cut him off. "We have enough water, I know best!"

"Yes, I know," he continues, matching my tone. "The stream runs north too. We can stay together instead of you bushwhacking alone."

As I bandage my cut as I wonder what hurts more: this self-inflicted wound or to admit, I've "learned" this lesson before.

Fast or Far

An old African proverb says: "If you want to go fast, go alone. If you want to go far, go with others."

The achievements we set out to accomplish, the big dreams and big goals, can rarely be achieved alone. We need healthy teamwork to get there.

Entrepreneurs and intrapreneurs tend to have a little less empathy compared to others. We also naturally shoulder risk a bit easier. I think these two traits are linked. We often don't care a great deal about the consequences that affect us personally and we don't immediately see how our actions affect others.

We do, however, care a great deal about gaining the admiration of others.

It can be very helpful, therefore, to intentionally watch our story from someone else's perspective from time to time.

Okay, I can hear you saying, "I'm supposed to care what others think of me?" Of course! If we truly didn't care what others thought of us, we wouldn't share love with anyone. The common bit of advice, "Forget about what others think" is meant for those who lack principles, insecure people with no compass.

I'm not suggesting you try to over please everyone, all the time. There is a big difference between asking "What do they think of me?" and "How am I affecting those around me?" One is selfish and the other is selfless.

It's healthy to take a quick snapshot of yourself from someone else's perspective. If they are writing the story about me as the main character, is it a story I'm proud of? Self-awareness is key for promoting healthy teamwork.

We tend to think the power of teamwork is mostly for the distribution of labor, but a healthy team can collectively obtain a much more complete vision of the path, the problems, and the solutions during all phases. We all see things differently and have wildly different ideas. A healthy team leverages this power.

During times of growth, companies often hire more people to simply "get more done". But unless everyone on the team ultimately agrees to go in the same direction, more people usually result in more complexity and resistance.

Again, in the context of business, it is much wiser to spend the time needed finding the *right* people, and then embrace the phases of story acceleration in a healthy rhythm of design, build, reflect, change, repeat. All together. All invested in every phase.

This can also be described as: Write the story, Find the moral, Tell the story, Repeat.

In a team, this pattern of improvement comes naturally when we embrace the incredible power of accountability.

Accountability is the intentional process of showing the team the value we bring to the collective.

Accountability is like an archway of bricks: together they have great strength and suspend entire bridges for centuries, but if one brick falls away, the whole structure crumbles.

Effective growth comes from the balance of courage and humility. Accountability forces both courage and humility. Courage to face the pain of work and conflict, and then humbly account for the areas you succeeded or came up short.

The golden rule is key here. Treat others how you want to be treated.

We want others to be kind to us, so we must be kind. We don't want others to talk about us behind our backs, so we must not gossip. We want people to believe the best about us, so we must be eager to give grace.

Think of a team like a body made up of unique, functional parts. Healthy team members see the value of protecting their arm, their foot, their leg.

However, we must also be completely committed to the effectiveness of our team. If a cancer persists, we must be courageous to cut it out when it becomes clear it's our last resort. Team leaders are faced with this question all the time. "Will this person improve their behavior? When do I need to let them go for the sake of the team?"

I don't subscribe to the old saying "hire slowly and fire quickly." I think if you have hired slowly then you should be able to fire slowly. Cutting someone from the team should be seen as a very serious last resort, like an infection that is so bad, an amputation is necessary to live. Firing quickly without a good amount of healthy coaching will only lead to your team feeling unsafe.

If the team member shows a commitment to accountability, there is hope. If not, let them go.

It's more important to coach team members on their continual commitment to accountability rather than performance. Performance will accelerate naturally once a team starts to enjoy progress made from accountability.

If anyone refuses to be accountable, they do not belong on a team. A team by its nature is interdependent which requires accountability.

By the same token, if anyone refuses (over time) to hold others accountable, they also do not belong on the team. This one is usually much tougher because our modern age prefers comfort over courage.

One of the most powerful examples of courageous and humble behavior is habit 5 in the *7 Habits of Highly Effective People* by Stephen Covey.

"Seek first to understand, then to be understood."4

The phrase can be broken down into a powerful two-part process:

1. We humbly pause our agenda and suspend our presuppositions and genuinely seek truth. By doing this first we are showing them love and respect which is exactly what we would want if the roles were reversed.
2. Once we believe we understand them we must have courage to explain our perspective and expectations. If they have felt our genuine love from part 1 they are much more likely to be receptive to part 2.

It's hard to overstate how important this is for healthy accountability among teams.

We cannot control the actions of others, but we can influence it over time. Not coincidentally the most effective and enjoyable influence comes from genuine, loving behavior.

The Power of Pause

In this chapter about **action**, I think it's important to also talk about the times when taking immediate action is very risky. When major conflict slaps us around out of nowhere, we often need to simply pause and do nothing but reflect on lessons we've learned before proceeding.

Have you ever typed up an email or text while angry about a situation? I certainly have. Hammering the keys like a prize fighter throwing 1, 2 combo punches, the message comes together with poetic justice. Then, just before sending I give it a final read, mostly to admire its power-- and that's all the time it takes. I cool down just enough to get a sinking feeling. Maybe I should sit on this before sending it. The scene of Homer Simpson buying a gun comes to mind. After the purchase the clerk informs there is a waiting period to buy bullets to which Homer replies: "But I'm mad now!"5

Quieting ourselves and reflecting is key for responding properly to conflict, especially people related conflict.

More than just a time to clear our head, we often need to rest in order to regain the energy needed for courageous response planning.

It's very important to accurately assess conflict within teams.

Teams that work hard together by nature have more conflict. Powerful growth comes from sprints of volatility. It's a good sign if your team wrestles often, as long as each person is willing to quickly take responsibility, and to restore admiration and appreciation of every other team member through genuine praise. At the end of every battle, we should recount the victory of lessons learned, laugh and smash our beer glasses together soliciting the power of the team and building our excitement for the next surge.

EXERCISE: Action & Resistance

Picking up where we left off, fill out Step 2 of the Story Acceleration Workbook. Pay special attention to the areas where you encounter resistance.

STEP THREE: NAVIGATE CONFLICT

I imagine he was lost in thought while stopped at that red light. I imagine his heart froze the moment his eyes caught the rearview mirror too late. I imagine the panic stiffening his body when the big truck made impact. No thoughts possible while his mind tried to catch up. His 1970-something station wagon spinning violently into the intersection. He never lost consciousness.

When it settled, he tore himself from the car, leaving his wife and 3 of his children in the wreckage. *"They were just napping in the back..."* the thought pulsed through his head over and over as adrenaline moved his wobbly legs toward the side of the road. There, he could see them- his other two sons, thrown from the car: little boys, one further away than the other. "Please God" was all he could utter as he reached the first, a screaming 3-year-old.

He picked up the boy and hurried back, holding the boy's bleeding neck and head while running. The mother reaches for her son, her maternal instincts pulling her out of shock. The father runs for his other son. He reaches the 6-year-old. Another wave of shock. The boy lays silently limp. The sight of the broken skull paralyzes the father.

Most of the moments that follow are remembered as a blur. The drunk truck driver stumbling around the scene. The police arriving. Five people were placed into the crowded ambulance: the father, his 10-year-old daughter, the two young boys, and another man.

On the way to the hospital, in the midst of his horror, while every cell in his body and soul silently scream to God for help, the father looks up at the man, the drunk, sitting there with them. They stare at each other.

Without explanation the father feels an indescribable peace take hold; the deepest form of peace, pouring into his being. A peace that shouldn't be there, but undeniably was.

While a heavy sadness lingered, equally strong was the unshakable knowledge that "All will be okay." An instant spiritual and emotional connection to a larger story, a story with many chapters, a story with a happy ending.

With their eyes locked, the father slowly felt his mouth open to speak to the man: "I don't know what you've done to my son, but I want you to know, I forgive you... and Jesus loves you."

My father's exact wording would not have been known throughout our life except that my 10-year-old sister heard it clearly while we laid there in the ambulance. He couldn't remember his exact words later, but my dad told us many times about his encounter in that moment with the "peace that passes all understanding".

That peace helped my father care for my mother in the season of grieving that followed. Though the jugular veins in my neck were almost severed, I was saved. My brother Jeremy passed away before reaching the hospital.

There isn't any amount of "I'm sorry for your loss" that helps ease the pain when you lose someone close. One day turns into another. You go through the mechanical motions of eating, sleeping, crying, and then you repeat it all. I don't remember most of it, but I remember we were numb, especially my mother.

It wasn't until a few weeks later that my mother had her peaceful encounter. One evening our doorbell rang, an older couple standing on our doorstep. My parents didn't know the couple but didn't seem phased at their presence. They learned we had mutual friends. They invited the couple in and sat at the kitchen table.

The couple proceeded to tell their story, about how they also lost a young son a few years ago. My parents broke down sobbing. Finally, here sitting in front of them were two people who understood their pain, two people who were able to keep going with life, and with strength enough to not only keep going but to come here to help.

Defying the statistics, these two people didn't divorce and here they were, able to smile, they didn't seem broken. It was all proof to my parents that life could somehow go on.

In only a few brief moments, the hope and energy created by this couple sharing their true story started an incalculable positive impact on my entire family and the untold numbers of people with whom we've shared this story.

Is that all it took for my parents to heal?

Of course not. Life rarely looks like one big lesson learned from which we move on without a scratch to live happily ever after. The conflict we experience in our (life) stories often come up over and over.

It was a key moment because it started remapping my parents' minds with hope. They felt the message the other couple was sharing. The message was this: "You can heal, you will laugh again, you will feel joy again... we did, and we do."

The thought of losing Jeremy would continue to be very painful, over and over. But with each session of grieving, each family member finished our grieving with thoughts about how great it was to know him for 6 years, how positively he impacted those around him, how much stronger we'll be as a family, how his story will help others keep from drinking and driving, how powerful the story of forgiveness will be for others.

This might at first sound like only sad thoughts which might continually point out his absence; but in reality, if we actively imagine the story having amazing outcomes for *others*, the mind and heart slowly starts to feel the joy of a more complete and powerful story.

When the story message is clear and powerful, others will retell it. Like a ripple from a splash, spreading outward through time. Unlike a pebble in a pond, however, a great story will grow in strength as people share it like a tsunami gathering momentum. This is why understanding the truth in the story is so important. It means the difference between gaining or losing power.

The more truthful the point of the story the more impact the story has, and the more energy there is to keep people telling the story.

I use this story in the chapter about conflict because I can't think of a more long-lasting painful conflict than losing a child.

Most of our fears are based on outcomes that won't happen. But this story serves as one of the worst possible outcomes that *did happen*, and we still healed. Each of my family members has gone on to achieve great things, partially because of the security that comes *only* from getting through conflicts.

What I am trying to say is this: Don't let fear hold you back. You will be okay! Most of what you fear won't happen and you will heal from what does happen, if you choose to. And the healing will leave you stronger, smarter, and with less fear.

History is full of heroes who came through the worst possible conflicts.

Thomas Edison

After being told he would never amount to anything by his schoolteacher, Thomas Edison went on to obtain more than 1000 patents in his life. I'm especially thankful for Edison because he invented the phonograph and the celluloid movie camera... the two devices that capture my two most favorite forms of art: music and filmmaking.

When attempting to create the lightbulb Edison failed somewhere between 1,000 and 10,000 times before he succeeded. Can you imagine failing at something 10,000 times? Instead of quitting, however, Edison tried and tried again until he achieved success. Think about that for a moment. No one at that time had ever seen an electric light bulb. Not only was it not thought possible, but it wasn't even thought of as necessary! The kind of dedication Edison had to believe it was both possible and important is nothing short of extraordinary.

Horatio Spafford

Almost a modern-day adaptation from the book of Job from the Bible, Horatio Spafford endured a series of events that should have broken him. The first two were the death of his four-year-old son and the Great Chicago Fire of 1871, which ruined him financially. He had been a successful lawyer and had invested significantly in property in the area of Chicago that was extensively damaged by the great fire.

His business interests were further hit by the economic downturn of 1873, at which time he had planned to travel to Europe with his family on the SS Ville du Havre. In a late change of plan, he sent the family ahead while he was delayed on business concerning zoning problems following the Great Chicago Fire. While crossing the Atlantic Ocean, the ship sank rapidly after a collision with a sea vessel, the Loch Earn, and all four of Spafford's daughters died.

His wife Anna survived and sent him the now famous telegram, "Saved alone..."1

Shortly afterwards, as Spafford traveled to meet his grieving wife, he was inspired to write a poem about his continued belief in God and his commitment to see a much larger, eternal story. Here are just two sections from the poem:

When peace like a river, attendeth my way,
When sorrows like sea billows roll;
Whatever my lot, Thou hast taught me to know
It is well, it is well, with my soul.

For me, be it Christ, be it Christ hence to live:
If Jordan above me shall roll,
No pang shall be mine, for in death as in life,
Thou wilt whisper Thy peace to my soul.

The full poem would go on to become one of the most influential hymns in history, helping to bring peace to millions of people ever since.

Viktor Frankl

I am particularly impressed with the story of Viktor Frankl.

An Austrian neurologist and psychiatrist. Born in 1905, his early life was difficult. During the first World War the family experienced bitter deprivation; sometimes the children would go begging to farmers.

In his high school years Frankl attended public lectures on Applied Psychology. He starts a correspondence with Sigmund Freud which is later published.

At 21 years of age, Frankl presented public lectures on congresses in Duesseldorf, Frankfurt, Berlin. For the first time he propounded the idea of a meaning-centered approach to mental healing, using the term Logotherapy, based on the Greek word logos for meaning.

While still a medical student, he organized special youth counselling centers to address the high numbers of teen suicides occurring around the time of end of the year report cards. In 1931 not a single Viennese student committed suicide.

After graduating Frankl became chief doctor of the "Suicidals Pavilion for Women" at the "Steinhof" Psychiatric Hospital in Vienna. In the following three years he gathers considerable diagnostic experience by attending to about 3000 patients per year.

He opens a private practice as Doctor of Neurology and Psychiatry only to have it shut down by the Nazi annexation of Austria. The Nazis force him to adopt the middle name "Israel" and call himself "Fachbehandler" (Jewish Specialist) instead of physician.

In 1940 he obtains an immigration visa to America but decides to stay to be with his elderly parents. Despite the Nazi oppression, he starts writing the first version of his book *The Doctor and the Soul.*

At the age of 36 he finds love. Frankl marries Tilly Grosser, a nurse he had met at the Rothschild Hospital. She became pregnant, but the Nazis forced her to abort the child.

As the totalitarian "3rd Reich" rises, Viktor and Tilly are arrested and together with Frankl's parents are deported to the Terezin Ghetto, north of Prague. The Nazis discard his unpublished manuscript. After half a year in Theresienstadt his father dies of exhaustion.

In prison, Frankl attends to the psychological crises experienced by the inmates of the Terezin camp by organizing a first response team for the shocked new arrivals. In his efforts to fight the danger of suicide.

Viktor and Tilly, and shortly later his 65-year-old mother, are transported to the Auschwitz-Birkenau concentration camp. His mother is immediately murdered in the gas chamber, and Tilly is moved to the infamous Bergen-Belsen camp. After a few days Frankl is selected for transfer to a labor camp. He is brought to Kaufering and later Tuerkheim, subsidiary camps of Dachau in Bavaria.

In the Tuerkheim camp Viktor comes down with typhoid fever. To avoid fatal vascular collapse during the nights he keeps himself awake by reconstructing the manuscript of his book Aerztliche Seelsorge on slips of paper stolen from the camp office.

In one memory, Frankl recalls a moment when marching in complete agony from the sores on his feet from broken shoes. He wrote about how in his misery, his thoughts had become fixated on the "endless little problems"2 of his life in the camp. These thoughts disgusted him, and he forced himself to think of something else. A picture came to mind of him giving a lecture of psychology to those at the concentration camp. At the moment of receiving this picture, everything that oppressed him before became objective from the perspective of science.

"By this method I succeeded somehow in rising above the situation, above the sufferings of the moment, and I observed them as if they were already in the past,"3 he writes. And then later states, "Emotion, which is suffering, ceases to be suffering as soon as we form a clear and precise picture of it."4

Frankl saw himself as the main character in a bigger, more important story. In later letters he describes this method as being of paramount importance in bringing him through it all.

On April 27, 1945 the camp was liberated by U.S. troops. Frankl is made chief doctor of a military hospital for displaced persons. Anxious to find out about the fate of his wife he embarks on the arduous journey to Vienna.

Within a span of a few days, he learns about the death of his wife, his mother and his brother who has been murdered in Auschwitz together with his wife.

In spite of this devastating news, Frankl continues to choose life. He takes steps toward living out the vision he saw by writing *Man's Search for Meaning* over 9 days. Though the writing process must have been a painful reliving of memories, he described it as rehabilitation!

To the reader, it is clear Frankel's excruciating struggles were all for a profound purpose. The book is a masterful example of ideas and beliefs seamlessly woven into powerful personal stories.

There are literally thousands more stories from history like these few. Stories of characters who fight their way through seemingly impossible amounts of conflict. And when they get through, the lessons they learn and the achievements they make are so great, their stories continue doing good long after they are gone.

We must not let the fear of conflict stop us from being active. If the heroes of the stories we loved let the fear paralyze them, there would be no achievement, no story to admire and tell about.

Embrace It

The third step to taking flight in your story is, **navigate the conflict when it comes, no matter how difficult**. Embrace it when necessary. See conflict for what it is: a vital part of your epic stories. Without it there is *no story*.

Seeing the hardship as a wave you can harness is the first step. Say to yourself... "Here it is, the meat of the story!" Let the conflict excite you to become triumphant and *understand that one day it will be told to encourage someone else*. This is a superpower for pushing through hard moments.

With every conflict you conquer, the next will be easier because you will have gained the confidence; the deep understanding in your gut that you'll succeed. You have in the past. This naturally creates energy which is what accelerates us.

We see this play out clearly among immigrant entrepreneurs.

Did you know the entrepreneurship rate for immigrants is about twice the rate of the U.S.-born? Not only are immigrants more likely to build businesses, they go bigger! A study conducted by the National Foundation for American Policy discovered immigrants founded 51 % of the country's startup companies worth $1 billion or more as of Jan. 1, 2015. Each of these companies employed an average of 760 people.5

Why? Because compared to what they have already been through, business conflicts are trivial.

Friedrich Nietzsche, the German philosopher was right when he wrote, "That which does not kill me, makes me stronger."

EXERCISE: Conflict

Follow the prompts in the workbook. Continue to write out your daily achievement stories.

STEP FOUR: DEVELOP
CHARACTER

The characters of a story are a vital ingredient. Without at least one character there is no story. Every person is unique; therefore, every character uniquely flavors the story. Like colors on a painted canvas the characters of a story offer a special blended value when you step back and look how they are painted into the entire story.

The uniqueness of a character naturally gets our attention. Have you ever heard someone say, "What a character!"? A character's style is what we see first, but much more important than the visible surface, are the choices a character makes.

The greatest characters are carefully, and painfully, developed.

In your life story, you are the main character, the protagonist. Think of your employees, your co-workers, your family, your friends... they are all casts of characters in the stories of your life, and of course you are a character in their life.

In classic fiction there are many character types, not all of which are used in every story. The twelve most common are:

1. Protagonist - the main character (the hero)
2. Antagonist - the main resistor
3. Deuteragonist - a side kick
4. Tertiary characters - seen a few times without great consequence
5. Love interest - needs no explanation
6. Confidant - a trusted friend to whom the protagonist can tell anything
7. Foil character - someone who's characteristics contrast the protagonist
8. Dynamic character - someone who is constantly changing throughout the story
9. Static character - someone who does not change throughout the story

10. Stock character - a character type seen in many stories, a stereotypical character

11. Symbolic character - They represent an idea beyond themself

12. Round character - a dynamic character with a full backstory, complex emotions, and realistic motivations.

Many of these character types are stacked into one character in a story. For example, the Love interest may also be the Confidant, or a foil character (originally seen as a competitor) may turn into a deuteragonist (a sidekick).

Pay special attention to that last one because, in fact, all the best characters in great stories are Round Characters with rich backstories and complex emotions. It's only because of a lack of time that we can't explore every character's depth in a book or movie. But notice how it's a little different in a TV show.

Over enough episodes we learn more about the lesser character and find commonalities which allows us to relate and empathize. What at first seemed like a disposable tertiary character, becomes almost like a friend we are eager to spend more time with.

It's this same way in life. It takes time and intentional investment to find what we have in common with the characters in our life. It takes careful communication and vulnerability. It takes work. This is not often easy for us quick moving, entrepreneurial types.

For the sake of simplicity, I want to focus on only 4 character types so we can remember them more easily as we analyze where we stand with each.

They are:
The Protagonist
The Ally
The Guide
The Antagonist

It's helpful to know what character you are playing in their story and to work at absolutely crushing that role; doing the most you possibly can (within the limits of the role) to improve their story. But before we dig into your relationship with others, let's talk about your relationship with yourself.

The Protagonist (You)

There are two different definitions for the word character, yet they rely on each other implicitly. Merriam Webster Dictionary defines *character* as:

1. The mental and moral qualities distinctive to an individual
2. A person in a novel, play, or movie

Our personal character can be described as what we're made of: our strength of conviction, our ability to do the right thing despite fear and pain.

The hero can't, by definition, be a hero without making difficult choices (usually moral choices), which leads to achieving something, if only wisdom.

A main character's ability to make difficult choices and take action despite fear and pain is what attracts us to them. As humans, we are naturally drawn to the strength of a leader because we feel safer following their lead. Mirror neurons allow us to feel the love they are giving by relinquishing their selfish desires in favor of others.

Great stories need great characters, and great characters are always forged in battle. The external battles we fight are easy to see, but the internal battles are what truly make or break the character.

This may sound similar to what we covered in the chapter about conflict. That's because character is nothing without conflict of some sort to develop it. Your conflict is trying to forge you into a hero right now. The battles you have already won are what give you the strength to face the next obstacle.

Stated another way: when we don't see and feel any growth in the main character over the story, it feels like a total waste of their time and ours.

In our spirit, we instinctively know real growth comes from winning deep, heart wrenching internal battles. The external battles of a story are only designed to bring us face to face with our fear and pain so we can fight, win, reconcile, grow stronger, and make more of an impact.

In life, just like the amazing tales we hear, read and watch, the breakthrough needed for the external struggle can only be realized when the corresponding *internal* breakthrough is achieved.

In *Star Wars*, Luke Skywalker is basically a bratty youngster when we first meet him, frustrated he hasn't been able to make a difference, to give his story meaning. Over three films filled with struggle and strife, he learns to face his deepest fears and temptations (internal struggle) and ultimately do the one thing no one else in the rebellion can do to stop the empire: confront his father and the emperor. Only this will save his friends (external struggle) and save the way of life he believes in.

The best characters are nuanced. A great character, by the end of the story, should demonstrate the balance of confidence and humility. Seeing the flaws of a character is essential for us viewers to identify with them, but if they don't make the right choice in the end, we are disappointed, and the story loses power.

In recent decades, the "anti-hero" has become increasingly prevalent in pop culture. I think it's because they demonstrate the confidence to not give a crap what anyone thinks about them. They are often quiet, subdued, and unwavering. This "self-reliance" gives the appearance of strength.

For sure, we humans are attracted to confidence. But imagine if you were "friends" with an anti-hero in real life?

A friend who won't communicate, takes selfish action, is relentlessly stubborn, or puts zero effort into the friendship is not a friend. It's for this reason anti-heroes are always portrayed as loners.

Loners will never achieve their full potential. Big stories need people working together, and people need strong, loving influences in their life.

The weakest and most boring characters are passive and refuse to take action. Even the story of the stubborn stoic who can't be bothered with anyone (usually in the first act) only becomes interesting when circumstances finally crack his shell and he starts taking action. If he didn't, there would be no story. Just a portrait of a turtle, who is too "strong" to stick his neck out.

The most detestable characters are those who's insecurities tempt them to blame others or maybe to blame circumstances when things go wrong.

A strong character is a hero who takes extreme responsibility for their actions or lack thereof. The most secure characters can absorb the weight of ownership as needed.

The Crash & the Con

"F*ck" I exclaimed without thinking, and I almost never swear. Smoke and fluid were pouring from the radiator of my dad's Toyota 4Runner, which was still shaking from the impact. Through the cracked windshield I could see the front end was completely smashed in.

Seconds before, I had failed to brake in time at a red light. It had just rained, and I slid about 30 ft into the back of a Jeep.

I looked over at my passenger, a friend my same age. At least I thought he was my friend. In a weird flash of emotions, I was both relieved and frustrated seeing he wasn't hurt. Only a few days earlier I found out my girlfriend wasn't interested in staying together but seemed to enjoy spending more time with this friend. I was his ride, and we were meeting a group of friends where I knew she would be. I had been lost in thought about the two of them; barely paying attention to the road.

As I climbed out to survey the damage, I could still hear our recent phone call bouncing around my brain like a pinball.

Me: "You don't love me?"

Her: Silence.

Me: "You were lying when you said you loved me?"

Her: Silence

Me: "You're not going to say anything?"

Her: "Goodbye Jed." Click.

The driver and passenger got out of the Jeep and started laying into me.

"You son of a bitch!" the woman screamed. "You almost killed us!!!"

"I'm sorry," was all I could manage to squeak out.

The man held his neck in pain silently and walked around the jeep with an odd-looking limp. The sheriff and ambulance arrive. To my surprise, the couple refused the ambulance.

The sheriff happened to be my next-door neighbor. He asked me if I was okay and decided not to ticket me. After seeing who I hit, I think he suspected I would be punished enough.

"He's a known con artist," The sheriff whispered to me. "Sit tight."

Great. Of all the people I could rear end, I thought. My dad showed up at the scene looking like a ghost. He came straight to me to see if I was okay. I was embarrassed about totaling his truck but he didn't even seem to notice that. He just wanted me to reassure him I was okay. I told him I was. It never occurred to me how my dad must have felt given what he had been through when we were young. No, at this moment I was just fixated on myself.

"It's okay," my dad reassured me. "As long as you're not hurt."

Though he said the words, I could see my dad was visibly distraught. This hurt my ego even more. I felt about two inches tall. The sheriff took their statements and came back to us.

"What happened?" The sheriff asked me.

Suddenly, I'm drowning in a petri dish under the microscope. I stammer desperately while searching for embellishments, anything to relieve the pressure.

"I dunno. It's wet."

"How fast were you going?"

I remembered I was approaching 40mph, 5 miles over the posted speed limit.

"Maybe 25 to 30."

Instantly I feel the lie burn in my stomach like poison. But it was too late, now I was committed to painting the best picture of myself possible, trying to dig my way out of a pit of insecurity.

As the following minutes crawled along like molasses on that day in January, I don't remember the sheriff's questions or my less-than-accurate answers, but I do remember the look on the con artist's face 30 yards away. I could see his wheels spinning as he eyed me and whispered things to his nasty Karen here and there.

Sadly, my friend and I didn't speak much after that and not because of the accident, or anything he did. He didn't steal my girlfriend. They never got together. They were just friends. He was (and I assume still is) a good dude. And truthfully, she was (and I assume still is) a very nice girl. It could have simply been a healthy breakup.

But my lack of character in a critical moment not only ended the friendship uselessly, but cost both me and my father more time, money, and grief in the long run.

Two years after the incident we received notice the *woman* was suing us for $3 Million. She had supposedly gotten a hip replacement at some medical facility in NYC no one had ever heard of and had suffered "severe emotional and physical damages".

The day of the deposition I was very nervous. We all met at the law offices. On the way up the elevator the opposing attorneys compared notes about my father's insurance umbrella and (I kid you not) high-fived in front of us.

As I was being deposed, I did my best to remember what I had said in my statement to the sheriff. Question after question they kept coming back for blood. Any time I said "mmhmm" the attorney would dryly quip, "Is that yes, Mr. Burdick?" Too much time had passed. I just couldn't keep my story straight.

The insurance company decided to settle out of court awarding the "victim" $750K.

Over the years I have reflected on this story and drawn a few valuable lessons from the details.

Lesson 1: My own mind is weirder than I thought. I was harboring dangerous levels of bitterness toward my friend without even knowing it, and for no reason.

Lesson 2: Insecurity is dangerous. It tempts us to take our eyes off what's important (driving safely, telling the truth, etc.).

Lesson 3: Only a few quick words can create much larger, long lasting negative consequences.

Over time, learning lessons allow us to heal. We gain clarity from these lessons and ultimately the deepest understanding, that when we operate with a clear conscience, everything will ultimately be okay.

Great characters have character. They make principled decisions, maybe not at first, but they are on a journey of learning and growth. In the best stories, the main character must apply what they have learned in order to defeat the antagonist and the opposing forces.

This is especially true of the main character, the hero of the story.

In the former chapter about conflict, I mentioned a few heroes from history who made principled decisions in the face of fear, but none of these heroes were developed overnight. Their impressive strength and life achievements came from untold amounts of action, choices, conflict, and lessons learned, which compounded their growth over a lifetime.

There are moments which act as catalysts, spurring us forward faster, higher, than normal. Often these growth spurts are not comfortable and come from necessity, sometimes even crisis. Thankfully our life is usually quite long, with many chapters, many chances for redemption, rest, reflection, and recovery.

Often, we don't naturally feel the larger progression of the story while living out a chapter. We tend to *over* feel the weight of our success or defeat in the moment when we should really be thinking about the larger story. The chapter is important, but the long form journey of growth is paramount!

We often need this amount of time to develop as a hero, but we can in fact be heroic immediately! Right now, today, you and I both have opportunities to take action and build a more meaningful story no matter what lemons life handed us, or how checkered our history.

We need to be both intentional about planning heroic action and be ready to respond heroically when an opportunity suddenly presents itself.

Unlikely Hero

On the afternoon of September 4, 2015, a man in a tattered dark-green jacket and baggy shorts suddenly turned violent inside the Cathedral in São Paulo, Brazil. For no apparent reason, he drags a young woman, Elenilza Mariana de Oliveira Martins, violently from the pew where she was praying. In a flurry of chaotic grappling, he manages to get her into a headlock as they reach the exterior steps of the church.

Gripping her as a human shield, a gun can be seen clenched in his hand. The panicked woman tries to escape his clutches. He shouts at the crowd of onlookers, swinging his gun wildly with deranged malice.

In a distracted moment she wriggles free and begins to run, but the man dives on top of her, pinning her to the ground with his knees.

The crowd is frozen with fear as the surreal scene unfolds in front of them.

Suddenly out of nowhere, another man emerges seemingly from thin air. His name is Erasmo Francisco Rodrigues de Lima, a 61-year-old homeless man known in the area. He has the advantage of surprise, sidling in from the assailant's blind spot. Without a moment of hesitation, Francisco tackles the much younger maniac, and the woman breaks free and runs.

The psycho fires once at the woman but misses. He then turns his gun on Francisco and fires twice into the elderly man's chest at close range.

The selfless and homeless hero stumbles backward and slowly crumples into his final resting place at the doors of the cathedral. Now exposed, a hail of bullets from local police instantly drops the evil man, ending his life and forever marking him a cowardly murderer.[1]

Two men lay on the steps bleeding out, similar in outward appearance, but their final legacies could not be more starkly contrasting. In fact, they were both homeless, they both had a long history of hardship. They both had years of destructive choices involving crime and abuse. Both men had spent the majority of their life in despair, neither able to enjoy the long-lasting fruits of compounding growth. But in this one moment, this one final act, one of them died a villain and the other a hero.

The Tightrope

As we transition to discussing your relationship with other characters in your life, I want to draw your attention to something very important. As you can tell from the writing so far, I believe self-actualization is of great importance, but *why*?

Becoming the best and most effective version of ourselves sounds like the ultimate key to fulfilment, but it's the love we give away that is most fulfilling. Emerging victorious from internal battles means more than simply growth for ourselves; in fact, it can be just as important for others in our life, depending on how we share our stories.

Ultimately, learning lessons and growing as a person allows us to better help others, and there is no greater sense of purpose than when we can help others *while* enjoying the fruits of our personal growth.

This is why so many entrepreneurs find themselves "teaching" more and more over time, rather than keeping the lessons they have learned to themselves. In fact, that's why I am writing this book. I want to share what I have learned, and I am excited to see others write more powerful stories with their lives.

I like to picture a character's journey as a tightrope walker attempting to walk the line above a cavern of apathy. The wire is called conflict. He is holding the long balancing stick. One side of the stick is the title "Love for others". On the other end of the stick, "Love for myself". Without both, the tightrope walker cannot balance himself while carefully, slowly, advancing through conflict toward his goal.

We are intensely motivated by our own interests, but we must not become unbalanced with either selfishness or "people pleasing." Fulfillment is achieved from becoming increasingly more effective at the role we play in our story *and* others' stories!

You are the protagonist in your own life story. What role do you play in their story? Are you an Ally, a Guide, or an Antagonist?

The Ally

An Ally is willing to help us, and we help them. From the deepest relationships like a confidante or love interest, to the tertiary characters, like that Bank Teller you kind of recognize, the key ingredient is a willingness to help in some way.

Some of the most important Allies are, of course, those with whom we live and work, and our closest friends outside of work. The amount of time we spend with these characters should be reason enough to improve the relationships intentionally and continually.

Allies are often friends, but not always. If you identify an Ally who is not really a friend, take steps to become true friends. This will always improve both of your stories!

In the past, I have had team members and clients in business who were Allies, but also "foil" type characters. Their style and communication habits annoyed me, maybe because they are so different from me.

By default, I didn't find myself wanting to spend time with them outside of work and consequently, our warmness would often plateau to the minimum viable level needed to get by. But I have also seen where intentional investment into these relationships yielded amazing dividends over time!

For example, Votary had a client who became an actual long-term partner once we spent more time together and found common values. There have also been a few employees who I thought didn't like me, until it became clear I simply needed to ask more questions and include them more.

Today I am so happy these relationships improved. We went from being tertiary-like characters, having little consequence on each other's lives, to becoming strong Allies, significantly moving each other's stories further and enjoying the process together.

These private stories I am vaguely describing, help remind me to continually invest into the other relationships in my life, even after painful setbacks.

Setbacks are not uncommon. I have had confidantes betray my trust and pass on information I wish they hadn't, and in truth, I have done the same thing to others who confided in me.

It can be difficult to rebuild trust after betrayal, and it is certainly wise to guard yourself from future exposure, but we must try to find other ways to improve the relationship *while* being okay with the fact that they may not allow progress past a certain point.

As I have said, strong Allies are vital for crafting the most epic life stories. In our business, we had a very clear and obvious surge of growth (which we are still experiencing as of this writing) when we shifted our focus from simply seeking transactions, to fostering actual long-term partnerships.

We did this with our paying customers and the community of filmmakers we work with as subcontractors. When we leaned into improving their lives (their stories), our story became far more profitable and meaningful!

Pay close attention to improving your Ally relationships and I promise you will see astounding acceleration and feel more joy in the process.

The Guide

The guide is someone who has been through it and lived to tell the tale. The guide is often an elder leader who has the wisdom and insights needed for the journey. They may not know everything about the specific challenges at present, but their history gives them unshakable confidence. Their stories have shaped the principles by which they live. It's a caring mother, a loving father, a mentor, and a teacher.

A few examples from great stories:
Aslan (Narnia)
Obi Wan and Yoda (Star Wars)
Gandalf (Lord of the Rings)
Jasper Palmer (Children of Men)
Alfred (Batman)
Kevin Flynn (TRON: Legacy)
Haymitch Abernathy (The Hunger Games)

If you are a parent or a grandparent, you are a guide to your children and your grandchildren.

If you are an aunt or an uncle, you are a guide to your nieces and nephews.

If you manage a department, you are a guide to your team.

And if you run a company, you are a guide to your organization *and* your clients.

Donald Miller goes into great detail about intentionally choosing to position your company voice as "the guide" because the customer is "the hero" in his wonderful book: *Building a Story Brand*.2

A good guide can truly accelerate our story.

For thousands of years, the wisdom of our elders was passed on to the younger generations through stories, to help accelerate personal growth. These stories were highly stimulating, and many became legendary moments of understanding. Can you think of a story your mother, father, or parent told? I can. I hope my children will effortlessly pass on my story lessons to their children along with their own.

If you watch a small child attempt almost anything, it can be painful not to jump in and help them. They waste so much time and energy in the process of figuring out the task, but of course, that is exactly what they need!

Then, once they can talk, it's common for parents (and managers) to instruct with a "Because I said so". If you are a parent, I'm sure you understand this temptation. I had amazing parents, but they said it too! I have certainly said it many times, usually when I am feeling impatient with my child asking "why" with an attitude.

The truth is, they do need to know "why". We all do. It's how our brain works. Taking the time to explain why with plenty of example stories is about the best investment of our time we can possibly make in the lives of those we lead and influence.

This is the role of the Guide.

If you are a guide for anyone, be the best guide you can possibly be. Remember, there is no official "guide" title or office. You have no right to command as a guide. You are a guide only as much as your followers will let you be their guide. Relentlessly pursue the life experiences needed to lead effectively. A good guide models the attributes needed to advance and overcome. A good guide has humility, a deep love for others, and guts!

I spoke a little about my grandfather earlier. He was a very powerful guide in my life. I admire him for many reasons but mainly because of how much he was able to change his life despite the deck of cards he was handed. His father was an abusive drunk. They had no money and no real assets but over the years my grandfather was able to start and build many businesses, truly changing his life and the lives of those around him.

I remember riding with him one day as we bounced around his different business locations. He was in his 80s but still involved as a leader and advisor with at least 6 different companies run by his sons. As I watched him interact with different managers, even as an old man, he had a calm charisma that drew you in. I can remember someone saying something like:

"Glenn, what don't you know?"

He snickered and quickly said, "Well, I only really have two things: a bit of understanding about people... and I have guts."

The statement stood out to me so profoundly. His tone of voice was so mild and secure.

My grandfather had lived through a lifetime of lessons learned from stories involving desperation, anger, drunkenness, the Great Depression, and of course World War II.

He was kind, thoughtful, and generous. But he was also cunning as a fox. His kindness was a choice. His kindness couldn't be mistaken for weakness. He asked a lot of questions. He ran toward conflict in order to solve it calmly and with unshakable resolve, not away from it, no matter what.

Many people are kind to others simply because it feels good, and we want reciprocation. But what happens when others don't reciprocate? A chain reaction: we don't get the feeling we were after therefore the brain doesn't get the dopamine it was looking for to complete the programming cycle. Instead, the result is heightened cortisol, the body's alarm system. This inevitably leads to the growth of a shell called bitterness, a defense mechanism ever at the ready.

Strong, important relationships require vulnerability, but it's possible to love others even when they don't love us back. Love is a verb. It's a conscious action... not a feeling.

To be sure, being kind gave my grandfather good feelings too, but the "good feelings" were not his aim. He was willing to make principled decisions as an investment. He wanted to enjoy an effective life story.

I think this grit and commitment to principle over feeling was more common in the former generations for a variety of reasons, but namely two:

1. For them, life was more about survival, earning pennies in hard jobs, toiling to grow food, and fighting in brutal wars

2. Because of this reality, the "love" that came from parents and other authorities looked very different... Instead of spending a lot of time being "mushy" with affection, the most loving thing they could do is teach their young how to survive... and survival took grit.

Today I feel privileged to have deep, affectionate relationships with my kids. I am often surprised at how much they are willing to share; it seems we can talk about anything. But I also want them to have grit and perseverance. I want them to enjoy the deep security that can only come from fighting through painful internal struggles. For this reason, I know I must not "save" them from the pain, but rather *guide* them through it with encouraging stories.

The Antagonist

We tend to picture the antagonist as a villain. An antagonist, however, is simply a character whose intentions conflict with those of the protagonist.

This could be a competitor, a legal opponent, an unreasonable customer, or maybe even a business partner who is hell-bent on going in a different direction.

Outside of work it could be one or more family members, or a "friend" causing deep resistance to your story.

This is tricky. It's very helpful to identify who is impeding your growth, yet it can be devastatingly destructive and unrealistic to simply cut them out of your life.

I am frustrated with business gurus who suggest divorcing from anyone who may be a negative influence. It really needs case by case analysis.

Ask yourself if the antagonists in your life are truly abusive or do they simply not understand or agree with your goals. Is there a long-standing pattern of destructive behavior, or is this simply a moment where brave communication is needed for growth?

Cutting and running from improvable relationships reinforce destructive long-term behavior and impede us from becoming effective heroes. Often, it's the exact opposite of what we need to grow and build the muscle needed for self-actualization.

This is especially true if we see a family member as an Antagonist. You can pick your friends, but you can't pick your family. Sometimes distancing from family is needed for a while in order to make progress. That is, unless we're talking about a spouse. Divorce should be reserved for extreme cases of abuse.

Let me take a moment to be a little more specific about spousal resistance.

If you see your spouse as the antagonist in your life *you must* devote an extreme amount of time and energy to fix this. Your spouse is your partner by definition and should not be an antagonist. Friction between partners is normal but left unresolved it festers and eventually turns into cancer.

If you feel your marriage has cancer, the road to recovery is beyond the scope of this book, but I will say this: At one point in your relationship, you were attracted to your partner, and they were attracted to you. You did things to express love for the other, even if they were small things. If it was possible then, it's possible to have it again. I say this from personal experience.

Very few marriages are completely irreparable.

For what it's worth, here's seven *GIANT* hacks I have found to improve my marriage:

1. Commit to improving it forever, no matter what. Unless they have been unfaithful or physically abusive, divorce is not an option.
2. Figure out your spouse's "love language" priorities and give love to those areas generously (in order!).
3. Most fights are about money. Figure out a money system you both agree on and stick to it.
4. In an argument, listen very carefully and calmly echo what you think you hear the other saying before calmly explaining your side. No matter how angry the other person gets, stay calm but not cold.

5. Be brave enough to apologize and ask for forgiveness for the areas you have screwed up. A lot of people say "sorry" but asking "will you please forgive me?" will truly pour medicine on wounds that want to heal

6. Continually improve your habits. If you know you keep doing something destructive, actively own it by admitting to the habit, and then work like hell to change it

7. In moments of peace, when you look at your spouse, intentionally list in your head what you love about them, then figure out a creative way to tell and show them what you love about them.

Okay back to talking about Antagonists...

Life is messy. Stories need conflict. Always try to resolve the conflict before moving on. If dealing with Antagonists was easy, we wouldn't learn much.

Intentionally improving our relationship with an antagonist is the right thing to do unless there is abuse.

If our kind and humble attempt to improve the relationship only yields a negative response (but not abuse), then simply elongate the time until the next attempt. Use the time to plan a more creative way to connect and build empathy in the next attempt.

When our attempt yields a positive response, shorten the gap to the next attempt and double down on positivity.

Be highly self-motivated and intentional about the effort you give to these challenging relationships.

Some of the most powerful stories have antagonists who turn into allies.

I'll never forget the feeling I had as a child the first time I watched the end of *Star Wars: Return of the Jedi*. There was the emperor, killing Luke in front of Darth Vader (Luke's father). When it appears that the Emperor and his loyal servant Vader have won. Luke says "Father, please." 3

Vader looks on, his black mask hiding all emotion. The emperor summons all his might for the final kill... Suddenly, Vader hoists the villain over his head, and walks him toward the death star energy shaft. Vader absorbs the force lightning into himself choosing his son over the dark side and sacrificing himself in this final act.

We spent 6+ hours over three films developing a fear of Vader. We needed him to be defeated. But in this powerful turn, we suddenly feel something more powerful than the satisfaction of revenge. We feel the loss of a character who was willing to die to save his son.

Les Misérables provides us with another example. In this story, Jean Valjean, a desperate fugitive, is taken in by a kindly priest who gives him food and shelter. That night, the opportunity to steal silver to better his position is too much for the fugitive to resist. He takes the items and hurries into the night only to be caught by the police and brought back to the priest.

The priest quickly confirms that he *gave* Jean Valjean the silver and says, "But you left so early, you forgot the best pieces. Why on earth would you leave the candlesticks, they are worth at least 2000 franks, why would you leave them?"

When the soldiers leave, the bewildered Antagonist says, "Why are you doing this?"

The priest quietly replies, "Jean Valjean my brother, with this silver I have ransomed you from fear and hatred. Now I give you back to God."[4]

Jean Valjean's heart is so moved, he is a changed man.

Turning an Antagonist into an ally is a very interesting and powerful problem to solve. It is surprising how often it is possible.

Of course, for this to work, it takes both sides to agree to the new relationship and there are plenty of cases where one side is simply not willing to change. I can think of a few battles I have had in different seasons where the antagonist refused to change no matter how much I tried to humbly find common ground.

It happens. In those situations, it's best to simply forgive them and move on. If circumstances don't allow you to move on (e.g., a legal battle) take the opportunity of "forced engagement" to keep extending the olive branch without sacrificing truth. You might be surprised at the outcome.

Life often has a way of forcing paths to cross again. Would you rather your paths cross as enemies or allies?

The final story in this section about an Antagonist is true, though it seems like a work of fiction.

Unlikely Allies

On a tense night in 2006, Andrew Collins, a young white Police Officer in Benton Harbor planned out another drug bust. He'd done it before and it always resulted in high fives, praise, and more of the attention he craved.

Determined, Collins arrested a black man named Jameel McGee. The only problem was, McGee was 100% innocent. Collins falsified the report, stealing, and planting drugs to incriminate his target.

"I got to a point where I didn't even view people as human anymore," said Collins. "They were almost prizes."[5]

McGee was convicted and sent to prison to serve a 10 year term for a crime he didn't commit. He lost everything. While in prison, Jameel McGee planned his revenge.

"My thought process in there when I first went in was to kill him whenever I got out,"[6] McGee remembers.

Meanwhile, the crooked cop kept sinking lower into criminal behavior which ultimately led to being caught with drugs in his possession.

On his daughter's birthday, Collins was indicted.

Collins admitted he falsified many police reports, including the one that put McGee in jail. Soon after Collin's guilty plea, McGee was exonerated of all charges and set free after serving 4 years and Collins went to prison.

While in prison, both men found faith. Collins shares, "The longer I was away from police work the more I kind of got the real me back... There's a lot of power in confession and the more I confessed what I've done I think the more of my own soul got back."[7]

After serving his time, Collins got out and ended up at the same Christian employment agency, called Mosaic which put them both as co-workers in the same cafe.

Collins shares, "He came up to me, shook my hand and said, 'Do you remember who I am? And I shook his hand and I said, 'I do.'"[8] He anticipated that something bad was about to happen.

"At that time, in my head, I'm thinking, hit him! Hit him! Hit him!"[9] McGee recounts.

But McGee chose not to hit the Antagonist standing there in front of him. Collins admitted all he had done with no excuses and ended with a deep apology.

"That's all I needed to hear,"10 McGee said. He forgave Collins then and there.

After receiving McGee's forgiveness, Collins broke down crying. "I just started weeping because he doesn't owe me that. I don't deserve that,"11 said Collins.

The two not only continued to work together but grew so close Jameel admitted that he loves his best friend, Andrew. They now do speeches and presentations together about the power and importance of forgiveness.

"I didn't forgive for Andrew's sake, or for my sake," McGee states. "I forgave for 'our sake.'"

Read their whole story in a book called *Convicted: An Innocent Man, the Cop Who Framed Him, and an Unlikely Journey of Forgiveness and Friendship*.6

What are you?

Here's a few tough questions to answer: Are you an antagonist in someone else's story? Whose progress are you thwarting?

With whom do you have significant or continual conflict? Why?

Even if you don't see yourself as the Antagonist in their story, what matters is how they see you. Do they see you as the antagonist? Why?

What can you do to become Allies?

EXERCISE: Character(s)

If you haven't already, download the Achievement Story Workbook Complete the three prompts to the exercise named Character(s). Continue your daily stories.

SECTION SUMMARY

As I mentioned in the preface about the Story Acceleration concept, Stories have two power phases: writing the story and telling the story. This first section has been all about writing better stories with your life. Smaller chapters will ultimately lead to a life story, making it awesome.

Again, meaningful stories come from leaning into the process of every step i.e., characters attempting to achieve goals through action, navigating conflict, and developing character in the process.

Now we move on to phase 2 where we find the moral through reflection, we plan what we will do better in the next pass, and we tell the story in the most authentic way possible.

Part Two:

Tell the Story

We did the work; we wrote the story! Whether our story was written yesterday, or has been decades in the making, we must now find the moral in order harness the wind's energy and begin to rise. From there, we choose the most effective delivery, and make the adjustments necessary for our next revolution around the Story Flywheel.

Your story is like a gold bar. It contains real value.

The story's lessons can be given freely, but we have to choose to tell them, and they must have ears to hear.

If we are too insecure to tell our battle stories, we miss out on the growth and acceleration available from the telling phase.

Similarly, if we choose to tell our stories but fail to be authentic, and instead "spin" the details, we're cheating ourselves and those who would benefit from hearing our story.

Unlike the front row seat from which we watch a hero in a good book or movie, our lives are rarely on display for all to see and judge. This is especially true in business. Our network doesn't automatically see us struggling with thoughts and fears in the dark of the night when the demons are burying us with anxiety.

They also don't see when we are quietly weighing the pros and cons of shutting down a department, pivoting, confronting a team member, or firing a problematic client.

By and large, our business life is private and that's not all bad. Remember the two halves in the power cycle of a story: writing then telling. If a story is still being written, it's not yet time to tell it.

However, those who choose to give the world a front row seat, can and do experience amazing growth, if the stories are authentic.

As we journey through the larger stories, smaller micro stories can be leveraged, too. This steady stream of episodic storytelling is incredibly powerful for building trust in the market if we are humble and vulnerable.

Unfortunately, the world of business has had decades of bad habits relying on the inauthentic "spin" in sales, marketing, PR, and internal politics. It's easy to fudge a few embarrassing details or simply omit them, which of course keeps us in a positive light.

Humans crave authentic stories.

Individuals and organizations who bare their soul and explain the dirty details of conflict, missteps, and the nuance of lessons learned, and celebrate the wins, stand out as strong and trustworthy.

The engagement formula is simple: Characters + Conflict = Curiosity.

Merely presenting ideas or opinions is not telling stories. While opinions are in stories, there is no curiosity without characters and conflict.

A compounding energy effect happens when we write the story, live the story, and then tell the story.

With this in mind, let's continue into the fifth step of Story Acceleration.

STEP FIVE: THINK AUTHENTICALLY

What value can something have if it is not authentic? I'm sure that many miners in the gold rush of the 1800s felt the blast of serotonin while panning for gold by the river. Their fingers cold, their bones tired; but then, there in the water, shiny metal flakes. The higher they got, the harder they fell when realizing the flakes in their pan were pyrite, a mineral known as "fool's gold." Similar in appearance but worthless in reality.

A giant shiny rock on the finger of an elegant woman can make you wonder, "Could it be a real diamond"? Or is it cubic zirconia, which is indistinguishable from a diamond to the naked eye.

At the time of this writing there are 577 episodes of *Pawn Stars* on the History Channel, but you only need to watch one to see the main conflict. Someone strolls into the shop with a historical artifact in hand. They carefully unwrap it as they tell the item's tale and how they got it. The rarer the item, the more the shop owner desires to buy it, but he has to figure out one main thing: Is it authentic? Is the story being told about the object true or false?

If it's true, the item has great value. If it's fake, it's worthless.

Counterfeit

Han van Meegeren was a Dutch painter born in 1889. As a child he became enthralled with the work of the artists in the dutch golden age and he worked tirelessly to become one of the greats himself. His father greatly disapproved of this and is even rumored to have forced Han to write a particular phrase, hundreds of times: "I know nothing, I am nothing, I am capable of nothing."[1]

Still, Van Meegeren pushed on. He studied under Bartus Korteling who had been inspired by the famous Johannes Vermeer. Korteling showed van Meegeren how Vermeer had manufactured and mixed his colors in the 1600s.

Through years of study and work on his craft, Van Meegeren developed an acute skill for painting in the old style similar to the masters, but critics denied him the validation he craved. It was said that his gift was an imitation and that his talent was limited outside of copying other artists' work.

One critic wrote that he was "a gifted technician who has made a sort of composite facsimile of the Renaissance school, he has every virtue except originality."[2] In response to these comments, van Meegeren published a series of aggressive articles in the monthly magazine De Kemphaan. He raged against the art community together with journalist Jan Ubink and in doing so lost any sympathy from the art of his time.

After his marriage ended from infidelity, he remarried an actress who went by the stage name of Jo van Walraven. She had been formerly married to an art critic and journalist.

Together, they decided upon a new venture to prove them all wrong. They moved to the south of France to start over. Van Meegeren poured over the biographies of the Old Masters, studying their lives, occupations, trademark techniques, and catalogues. From the years 1932 to 1937 van Meegeren worked alone, quietly shut away in his studio painting the masterpieces by which he would forever be remembered.

What original works of art were these famous paintings? Forgeries.

He crafted "missing" works by Frans Hals, Pieter de Hooch, Gerard ter Borch, and of course his favorite, Johannes Vermeer. Vermeer had not been particularly well known until the beginning of the twentieth century; his works were both extremely valuable and scarce, as only about 35 had survived.

The forger bought authentic 17th century canvases and mixed his own paints from raw materials using old formulas. He created his own badger-hair paint brushes similar to those that Vermeer was known to have used.

But the oil paint was a much more difficult problem to solve. Oil paint takes decades to harden. So, after completing a painting, van Meegeren would bake it to dry it quicker, but the paint would brown and burn. After a series of painstaking tests van Meegeren found that by mixing phenol formaldehyde (bakelite) the paint could be instantly "aged" with the perfect look. He then rolls it over a cylinder to increase the cracks. Then, he would wash the painting in black India ink to fill in the cracks.

He had finally become a master.

Through a web of lies and a network of agents, van Meegeren begins selling the forgeries. No Vermeer paintings had been found in centuries, then suddenly, they started turning up every few months. Every collector in Europe desperately wanted one of their own.

World War II raged, and in the time when most were losing everything they had, including their lives, Han van Meegeren amassed a fortune of more than 7.5

million guilders which is more than $30 Million USD today.

One of the greediest collectors of the day was Hermann Goering, the No. 2 man in Nazi Germany. He was famous for his collection of looted paintings. During the German occupation of the Netherlands, one of van Meegeren's agents sold the Vermeer forgery *Christ with the Adulteress* to Nazi banker and art dealer Alois Miedl.

Goering traded 137 stolen paintings for this one Vermeer, the new prize in his collection.

Van Meegeren's health had declined and so had the quality of his work. He chain-smoked, drank heavily, and was addicted to morphine-laced sleeping pills. However, there were no genuine Vermeers available for comparison since most museum collections were in protective storage as a prevention against war damage.

Christ with the Adulteress, the painting sold to the Nazi, became van Meegeren's undoing. After the war,

Miedl the Nazi art dealer was caught and confessed to where he acquired it.

When the police knocked on the door of van Meegeren's mansion in 1945 to question him about the issue, the forger didn't have a very convincing answer.

He was arrested and charged with fraud and with aiding and abetting the enemy. Held in the Weteringschans prison as an alleged Nazi collaborator and plunderer of Dutch cultural property, Hans van Meegeren faced the death penalty.

To save his own life, he confessed to forgery. But no one believed him.

And so, Van Meegeren was forced to prove his skill by painting his last forgery between July and December 1945 in the presence of reporters and court-appointed witnesses: "Jesus among the Doctors" in the style of Vermeer.

After completing the painting, he escaped the death penalty and was released from prison but was still to be tried for forgery and fraud.

In a strange twist, during his very public trial van Meegeren was able to deliver a compelling story and win the public's affection. He exclaimed his love for Holland, and what better way to show patriotism, than to con their greatest enemy.

Was it true? Was he a patriot, intentionally profiting from his enemy's naivitae, or simply a broken man cursed by the words of his father ? Forever crippled with insecurity and unable to stop seeking approval with more forgery?

He was sentenced to one year, but he never served a day. At the age of 58, the abuse of drugs, alcohol, and stress, finally caught up, and Han van Meegeren, the most talented and profitable forger known in history, died of a heart attack shortly after filing for bankruptcy.

After his sentencing van Meegeren told one reporter, "I'm sure about one thing: if I die in jail they will just forget all about it. My paintings will become original Vermeers once more."[3]

He believed his work was so true it would transcend the lie from which it was founded. But sadly, just like the art he forged, the delusion to which he held, was also false.

Nothing in life is valuable unless it is authentic. In fact, value and authenticity are interchangeable. They share the same curve on a graph.

In storytelling, our goal should be to truly connect with those who will listen and benefit from our stories. When we tell a truthful story, complete with the vulnerable details, we accelerate ourselves and our listeners in a positive direction.

If we lie (to others or ourselves), we accelerate in a negative direction.

While it might sound easy to navigate, the temptation to embellish is a strong opposing force. We storytellers know it well. It's just so easy to sprinkle a few small gold stars here and there, and of course, leave out a few embarrassing details... but before you know it, the story is lacking authenticity and therefore, lacking value.

Embellishments are shiny little lies. They are far more sneaky than big lies because they don't feel wrong. They just feel like good packaging. They feel like they are helping the story.

Do you feel more moved when you watch a "true story" or read the real details in a biography? I do. When I see the words "based on a true story" at the beginning of a movie, I just *have* to look up the details when the film is finished. I am often disappointed by how much "creative license" Hollywood takes to make the story fit their desired plot points and emotional arc.

While it is true that a dramatic story is more compelling in the short term, it's important to remember that all our stories add up to a larger life story.

In the long run, authenticity outweighs drama. Authenticity builds trust. Authenticity is the tortoise, not the hare.

People know what is real and what is doctored, and this understanding dramatically affects their willingness to become allies i.e., friends, teammates, and customers.

Many organizations try to tell authentic stories internally but fall short when it comes to allowing the market to see vulnerabilities and lessons learned. Sadly, these organizations are operating with one hand tied behind their back, not realizing the full potential of their story. When internal team members see senior leadership who are open and willing to allow interesting, vulnerable stories to be told about transformation, the organization as a whole can feel the freedom of truth. This strengthens the culture with a deeper sense of meaning and security.

The habit of telling an inauthentic story comes from three possible scenarios:

1. Our story time scale is too short. We don't have enough data to figure out the true lesson, but we attempt to tell it anyway.
2. We didn't spend the energy necessary to follow a process and figure the true lesson i.e. laziness
3. Telling the moral will require more vulnerability than our pride allows. i.e. our ego is in the way

(Notice the villains, laziness and fear, in 2 and 3; they are always lurking.)

The secret superpower to discovering and overcoming these three habits is intentionally building an accountability structure around the process of *reflection*.

The Power of Reflection

The importance of this process cannot be overstated. Reflection is used throughout the entire second power phase of *telling* the story, but especially prior to finding the moral. We're now past the moments when the story was being written, when we were fighting conflict and couldn't see the forest from the trees.

We can now look back and examine every step of the story, every choice that was made. What was our mindset? What did we achieve? Did we go astray anywhere? Could we have been more effective?

Reflection allows us to set the table with the data needed to hypothesize "Why?" and "What will we do differently next time?"

It allows us to feel the value of our choices.

If we skip this process, we're ignoring the quest for growth. Almost inevitably, we will plateau, and or become resentful and or unmotivated.

A great example of this can be seen in the marvelous work of fiction, *It's A Wonderful Life* (my favorite film). George Bailey wanted nothing more than to leave Bedford Falls and make something of himself. But every opportunity to leave was paired with the difficult decision to ignore the needs of those he loves. Each time, George chose to put the needs of others ahead of his own desires but failed to reflect and feel the good in these decisions. Consequently, he became resentful and stuck in a false paradigm about his lack of value. Clarence the Angel takes him on an intense journey to see the world as if he had never been born.

No one knows him. No one can share his memories. Everything is different. Essentially George was allowed the gift of experiencing a wildly vivid type of forced reflection. He can now see the meaning of his life choices so far.

With this new paradigm, George finally surrenders and pleads with God to let him live again.4 Watch the movie if you haven't; it's truly a masterpiece.

As we grow older, the lessons we learn will give us wisdom, *unless* we refuse to learn from them. In that case, life must push us to learn the lesson again and again, like a broken record skipping back to the same spot over and over, a maddening lack of progress.

Reflection keeps us honest and grounded. It allows us to continually check our assessments. It allows us to "go back there" in our minds and hearts and feel the situation again.

Honest reflection also gives us empathy for those who are about to march into a battle we've already fought.

We need this empathy to craft our stories into beautiful gifts. If our listeners believe they are receiving something that will truly help them where they are, our stories will connect, and they will eagerly unwrap these gifts like a child at Christmas. The packaging is important to engage them with delighted suspense, but it's not the gift.

The gift is the moral to the story along with the belief it will have value *in their life*. It's something they can take with them and use when needed.

The key phrase there was "in their life." By default, our stories will sound like a tale that applies only to us, unless we paint a compelling picture using *authenticity*.

Fast vs Strong

I have used the words "accelerate" and "acceleration" a lot in this book because we're emotional beings. When we feel momentum, it becomes easier to make even more progress. It's a fact. In this chapter on Authenticity, however, I feel a deep need to also explain something very important: a false sense of progress is deadly.

Imagine building a house on the beach. You skip all the time and effort of mixing concrete and pouring a foundation and simply rally your team to frame it up in *one day*. Everyone stands back in awe and admires the building. The neighbors all around start buzzing about how fast you were able to create something so beautiful. They become inspired and start building their own beach homes. "Tomorrow we're going bigger!" you exclaim.

But tomorrow, the house is gone. A storm came in the night quickly reducing it to a heap of useless rubble. You have to start over.

Authenticity is all about growing *stronger* which then lets you go *farther* in the long run.

Authenticity requires vulnerability. There is no way around it. The reality of life is that the truthful details of our experiences are nuanced with strange little moments of trial and triumph. When retelling an account, it can seem so obvious what the right move should have been and our desire to tell a black and white story might tempt us to skip the shaky details. Exposure feels uncomfortable. It often feels like these little vulnerabilities are reducing the power in our stories. Won't people see us as weak or incompetent?

The truth is some will. Authenticity exposes our humanness which can turn some people off (at least temporarily). But it also builds trust in the long run!

The pain of authenticity makes us better. Over a long enough scale of time, not only will lost allies return, but they become evangelists. *Their* followers often come with them!

Authenticity helps us grow stronger, faster.

An authentic story is not just a story that shares the dramatic details; it continually draws attention to the actual conflict, the actual fears, the actual missteps, and the actual lessons learned. If we're still unsure of the true lessons, we must state that clearly or simply choose not to tell the story yet.

Consider the impact authentic storytelling has on your own personhood as well. Authenticity is the seed that grows into peace. Those who navigate life from a deep state of peace enjoy a fullness which is hard to explain.

When most people say the word happy, I believe they really mean peaceful. The deepest inner peace is, in fact, more spiritual than psychological. While my exact beliefs about the spiritual realm are outside the scope of this book, I welcome you to ask me for these details any time. For now, suffice to say that authenticity is a great promoter of peace, so tell the most authentic stories possible, especially to yourself.

Hear me clearly, I am not suggesting that your story must contain dramatic woes for it to have value.

Whatever the truth is, center your story around that. Watch out for the trap of humble bragging and over-glorification. Humble brags are not vulnerable and therefore not authentic. Humble brags do not have empathy and do not connect with the listener.

If my friend Charbel had not humbled himself enough to explain his embarrassing lack of savings, mountain of debt, foreclosures, and all the painful details of his missteps, his story would have been sorely lacking in substance and power. He could have said something like "The stupid economy crashed and set us back" or worse, "If the damned greedy bastards of wall street hadn't taken on sub-prime loans..." Instead, he took total responsibility and explained the consequences in painful detail.

His tone and pace were empathetic to me and my current situation.

By doing this, his story was instantly authentic and carried the weight and power it should.

It's easy to underestimate how difficult this can be in the moment. It takes intention and force of will to fully own the problems of the story. It's incredibly tempting to blame or downplay our missteps. But a bond of trust is truly only built from empathy and relatability.

Say it to believe it

The stories we tell greatly shape how we *think*, and how we think determines our future.

Neurologists say that our thoughts can either be pictures or words. Pictures are hard to change but words are relatively easy.

With the stories we tell ourselves, we're continually injecting words into our brain and consequently shaping our beliefs.

It's easy to think this only applies to larger, self-aware statements but in reality, the smaller statements we make every day in autopilot are what really add up to shape our beliefs.

Our goal is to be authentic without surrendering the fight to the wrong thoughts. A powerful hack is to conquer two different types of statements:

1. Catch yourself and actively choose the best words about your identity like "I am..." or "I always..." or "I never..."
2. Catch yourself when you're about to complain about anything, even something small and simply don't do it, not even to "vent".

When we use the words "I am", we are literally programming our brain to believe something about our identity. And consequently, we act according to that belief.

I have a relatively healthy view of myself, but a phrase I'm often tempted to say is, "I'm not great at money management." Recently, I have been actively trying to replace that with, "It's been a struggle, but I'm getting better at money management."

Negative self-statements are as common as breathing in today's society. We all hear it all around us every day.

"Oh, I'm the worst at math"
"I have a terrible memory"
"I can't do that"

These are all telling a story: A tragedy.

At first it sounds like we're simply stating a fact-- isn't that being authentic?

No. "I am" is not time bound. It's a statement of what was, is, and always will be. And that's not authentic. We can never let historic evidence control future outcomes. That's called surrendering.
Imagine the different impact of these two statements on our brain: "I can't do this." or... "I'm struggling, but I'll get through this... what could help me right now?"

What we say about ourselves will lead to what we believe about ourselves. If you believe you are improving, you will keep improving. If you believe you are perfect, the wave of life will crash over you and suffocate your arrogance.

By sharing stories complete with the vulnerable details and transformative lessons, we become more secure, more caring, more relaxed, and more attractive.

Because I am a film editor, I can't help but wish I could show you two scenes from my life to further demonstrate my point here. I'll just have to describe them.

The first scene is me at 11 years old. I'm standing in the street with a zoologist and TV news reporter. I had just given an interview about a lynx I had spotted in our backyard. It had been quite a moment for me, locked in a staring game with the giant cat. The zoologist had been radio tracking the Lynx who had wandered about a hundred miles south from the Canadian border through the Adirondacks and into our little suburban neighborhood in Upstate, NY.

I was high as a kite from giving the TV news interview. After the cameras were off, I wanted the attention to continue. I showed off my amazing knowledge of big cats with the Zoologist who snickered at me as I tripped over the details. I attempted to amend one of my statements about Lynx mating patterns and the snicker turned into a full-blown burst of laughter between the adults.

A tidal wave of insecurity crashed over me and I walked away to sob by myself.

The second scene is me at 41 years old, very recent to the time of this writing. I'm in our conference room pouring over our "Story Acceleration" brochure with the Votary leadership team. While attempting to edit some of the copy out loud, I stumbled over my words while maintaining a tone of absolute strength and conviction. I sounded like Martin Luther King Jr. reading *Mad Libs*.

The team burst into laughter.

It was a vulnerable moment. I wasn't in a mood to joke. I was digging deep to find the wording for these important ideas! Their sudden interruption of laughter jolted me from my focused state.

Again, a wave of insecurity crashed; blood rushed to my face. But then I suddenly saw myself from their perspective, and it *was* really funny. As a quick defense, I joined in their laughter and repeated the joke with even more exaggeration.

Here is where I'd like to "spin" the story and say because of 30 years of growth, my insecurity instantly vanished. But in reality, it took a good five to ten minutes to shake it off by silently reassuring myself they weren't making fun of me. They love me, I just sounded ridiculous. It *was* funny!

This is only one of many times when I have had to recover from a group of people laughing at me. Some people have no trouble with this, but it tends to make me squirm under the microscope for a while.

As I write this, it doesn't feel *great* to admit my insecurity about something so simple as laughter, but it's the truth.

It's also the truth to explain how I have seen progress in this area over my life. For example, I've seen that if I fixated on their laughter and ribbing, I might become even more self-conscious and consequently start responding defensively, or not at all. But that's not a result of their actions; it's the result of *mine*.

Only I can decide to fixate on it or not. Only I can choose what to believe. Even when people are mean spirited (which is rare in my life) I can and have said in my mind: S*mile. Keep going, this will pass. Don't punch back. Show kindness. Plan your response carefully.* This has really helped me over time.

Notice how my story about my insecurities didn't end with the vulnerable bit-- it turned positive. It focused on the evidence of growth. It focused on "why" I should continue, discontinue, or adjust the action for next time.

Answering the question "why", is stating the moral to the story which is what we'll discuss in the next step. If I had never reflected or dug deeper for the lesson to learn and apply, chances are I'd keep overreacting emotionally and probably would have fired everyone by now.

EXERCISE: Authentic Insights

Complete Step 5: Authentic insights in the Story Acceleration Workbook. Continue to fill out the achievement story of each day.

STEP SIX: FIND THE MORAL

Swish swish swish. *What the hell is that sound?* I wonder while staring into black void of nothingness. I am struggling to hold on to any sort of cognition. Thoughts and feelings flutter in and out of my head at a blistering pace. I feel myself sucking air in and out. I can't seem to find enough air.

More thoughts strobe through my mind's eye like someone is pressing fast forward on the video tape of my consciousness. The sound grows louder. SWISH SWISH SWISH. *Where the hell am I?* I'm in a nightmare. This could be what hell would be like. But I'm not actually *in* hell... am I?

How did I get here? Was I bad?

I'm on a bicycle now, struggling to pedal away from the darkness but something is impeding me from making any progress. I look down at the lower half of my body and see roller skates strapped to my feet while trying to pedal the bike; they just keep slipping off the pedals. I'm falling.

Swishswishswish- the sound overwhelms me. *I'm dreaming,* I think. *Wake up.* My eyes snap open. I see where the walls meet the ceiling above my bed and nothing has ever seemed so terrifying.

I sit up in bed. I'm sweating profusely and shaking like a leaf. I'm in a hotel room on the edge of the Grand Canyon. I glance back up at the ceiling. It feels like a monster trying to swallow me. "Don't look at it," a voice says in my head. Is that my voice? I can't tell.

What's wrong with me? I try to stand up. I need to get to the bathroom. Again, I look at the corner where two walls meet the ceiling and almost lose all motor skills from terror. I have no depth perception. The walls are caving in on me. I can't breathe. Claustrophobic panic forces fight or flight.

I'm awake. What's wrong with me?

I get to the bathroom and spastically try to splash water on my face. It doesn't help... I just feel a more vivid and acute sense of the nightmare.

I pull my guitar out of its case by my bed and manage to play a chord or two. Maybe something beautiful will fix me.

"It's no use," the voice in my head whispers. "You're killing your parents."

My parents. I remember they are in the hotel room across the hall. What's happening to them? How am I killing them? I don't want them to die.

"You're letting them die!"

No, I'm not! I spring to my feet and exit the room. There, I can see their room. What's happening to them? I won't let them die. I yank on their door. It's locked. I keep trying the handle.

"It's too late. It's your fault they're dead!"

It's my fault? How could I have let this happen? No no no no no. What's wrong with me? Why did I do this? Maybe I can still save them!

"You can't."

What's wrong with this door? If only I can open this door I can save them!

"It's too late for them. Everyone is going to know what you did."

Why did I let them die? What's wrong with this door?

"You need to run. Or they WILL find you. They know what you did."

Yes, that's true. I can still run. I can hide. Where will I hide? They will eventually find me!

"You can run out that door down there, and off that ledge."

I look down the hall at the green exit sign hanging over the metal break away door. I remember the patio beyond the door on the edge of the Grand Canyon.

"It will be quick- just jump. Get it over with before they find you!"

I feel the adrenaline spiking toward my legs like daggers, preparing me for the run toward the door.

Wait. There is a spell on this door. I can undo the spell by running up the door and landing a backflip off it! I have to save them!

I take two steps back and then charge the door. My feet run up the door as if I am trying to spring up and out of an empty pool. As I lose momentum, I remember the magic backflip needed and I spring backward. My body folds in half as I land my neck and shoulders into the hardwood floor. I don't feel the pain.

If at first you don't succeed, try try again! SWISH SWISH SWISH

I know I can break this spell if I land on my feet. I charge the door again with more force. This time I snap my knees into my chest once horizontal and my body flips backward.

I come down hard, smashing the floor on all fours.

The spell is gone. No more panic. No more fear. No more guilt. I am suddenly sane again.

Swish swish swish. I realize it's the sound of blood pumping through my head and ears.

I look up at the still locked door and the reality of my psychological situation starts to set in.

I slowly stand to my feet and looked toward the other end of the hallway. There, I see a woman staring at me. I realize I am in my underwear. I recognize the woman from the day before. My parents had spoken with her, exchanging "where ya from's".

"Have you seen my parents?" I manage to ask her.

"I saw them walk over to the restaurant for dinner, I think they wanted to let you sleep."

I sheepishly limp back toward my room and try to escape the naked awkwardness. I try my door. Of course, it's locked.

"Are you okay, sweetie?"

This story might sound like a tale told by Hunter S. Thompson after an escapade with LCD. Maybe it just sounds like bad fiction. But it is, in fact, a true story from a trip I took to the Grand Canyon with my parents when I was 18 and no, I was not on any drugs.

Two days before this incident, my father and I went "indoor skydiving" in a vertical wind tunnel in Las Vegas. During the flight, my ear plug fell out and air pressure ruptured my eardrum.

Unbeknownst to me, an infection set in and my body had to fight with a fever.

I almost killed myself that day in the hotel, for no reason rooted in reality. The fever dream in which I was trapped had me convinced of a reality that wasn't real.

This experience had a profound effect on me. I have reflected on it many times throughout my life and it continues to teach me lessons.

The first lesson it taught me was how deeply connected our perception of reality is to the health of mind and body. From that point on, I wanted to take better care of myself to avoid ever getting sucked into that deception-filled, living, walking nightmare dimension again.

It also gave me great empathy for so-called "crazy" people you see on the street corner or the subway... you know, the type that continually mutter to themselves and glance this way and that. It made me realize just how different their reality (think mental state) is from mine.

This is not to say there is no absolute truth. On the contrary, it's because I believe there is absolute truth that my heart goes out to those who have a warped perception of reality.

But isn't that all of us? Don't we all have a different perception of what is real and why things are?

This is why continually seeking "the moral" to our stories is so important. It shapes our reality.

The "Why"

The moral is the heart of the story. It answers the most fundamental question asked in the story: "why?" Why does anyone do anything? Why did the main character go through those challenges? Her scars are all reminders of what happened, but what happened is meaningless without *why* it happened. The "why" is essentially the lesson learned.

When I think of "story morals", I immediately remember simple children's stories like Aesop's fables. Do you remember them? "The Tortoise and Hare," "The Goose and the Golden Egg," etc.

These stories were originally written to help adults grasp the practical importance of guiding principles but over time they have been relegated to being published mostly for children.

As we grow older it seems like we think of our stories as being more complicated and having more "gray" areas; but perhaps we fail to find clarity because we do not take the time and process the value of our choices.

Reflecting and finding the truthful lessons learned is the process of painting a map. The map needs details! The more we reflect on the motivations, the forks in the road, and the choices made, the more details we are painting into our map.

Continually asking "why" is an effective way to drill down and expose the details.

For example, while reflecting about a particularly difficult week I realized a few things: I was impatient a few times and I complained about someone... borderline gossip. Why? Why was I off my game last week? Well, I did stay up until 2am a couple nights, ate junk snack food before sleeping, and didn't do my positive morning routine.

Is that it? The lesson learned is if I stay up too late and eat junk, I am compromising my mental health? Yes, that could be true, but let's dig deeper.

Why did I stay up late? Because I had interruptions in the day which prevented me from hitting my deadlines, so I needed to work late to stay on track. Why did I eat junk food at 2am? Because I was hungry! Nope. I could have had a piece of fruit. The truth is, in my late-night state of feeling accomplished, I subconsciously justified the junk food reward. I didn't feel like slowing down enough to count the cost.

I might have been able to prevent the interruptions in the day by closing my office door.

These examples might sound over simplified, but I find there is almost always more than one lesson to be learned, and tactics to try for next time. The key is to reflect and ask why.

If I look at the bigger story, I see that when I allow myself to get out of balance with a few seemingly small compromises (staying up way too late, eating poorly) it can have a much greater impact than I think it will in the moment.

The lessons we learn from reflection should not all be negative. It's just as important, if not more important, to state what we believe we did right!
Celebrate the correct choices and deepen those positive habits.

Watch out for the trap of reflecting without critical thought. Many people just say "that happened" rather than figuring out the lesson. Your short-term stories should contain at least a hypothesis of "why".

It's not a lesson unless we learn. I am not suggesting that you dwell on things for too long. Simply go through your scheduled reflection time, dig into the "whys" and then arm yourself for next time. Just as with all the winds of life, there is a rhythmic balance which can be found here.

What about the situations where there is a lack of evidence to support the moral, should I simply not share the story yet? That's up to you to answer case by case. Sometimes it's best to wait.

But we've also seen, the more comfortable you become with authentic storytelling, the easier it will be to say in your story: "We're not 100% sure, but our gut is X and our plan is X... we'll see how this plays out!"

This is intentionally letting your audience come along with you on the journey. You are showing them a chapter of the story with a glimpse of what you believe the moral will be. This type of episodic storytelling is incredibly powerful for building trust. The storyteller is essentially saying "I don't have all the answers, but I am on my quest to find them." This requires confidence and humility, the two greatest ingredients for gaining influence.

If you study any good, scripted TV series, the pattern you'll see in the character journey is as follows: The story exposes their deep internal flaws, they take steps to heal, they grow, the plots change, the stakes raise, the character's reactions change, but they continue to deal with their flaws. Essentially, this cycle happens on repeat for the duration of the series.

Is it really any different in life? We grow and change, and conflict is always present. The most compelling stories boldly show these conflicts *and* the lessons we continue to learn.

Finding the moral to the story is a continual search for the lesson learned with every cycle around the story flywheel. We need to form enough of a moral hypothesis to at least test it's application; that is, try a new tactic the next time we encounter similar conflict. As we write new stories, new evidence should coax us to revisit old lessons learned and test them again for authenticity. This is how our lessons are refined and our growth becomes further optimized.

New Details in the Story

I don't remember the car accident where we lost my brother Jeremey. Growing up, I heard the story in bits and pieces a few times from each parent, and from my siblings. Each added a little more detail. By the time I was 16, I believed I knew all the pertinent points of the story. However, decades later when I asked more questions of my mother and sister, I came to learn something new and profound!

For years I had misunderstood the exact phrase my father said to the drunk while we all sped toward the hospital in the ambulance. I believed he had said, "I don't know what will happen to my son, but I forgive you." My sister Sarah gave me the correction. He had really said, "I don't know what *you've done* to my son, but I want you to know I forgive you."

These phrases communicate very different things. I had always wrestled with feeling like my father sounded a little weak in that moment. Now decades later, a father of five sons and one daughter, learning the words "...what you've done to my son" connected me to the personal pain and anger he felt toward the man. This made the forgiveness statement more powerful. It defies all logic and emotional reasoning. It could only be supernatural.

This truth brought new energy. I felt compelled to see if my siblings also knew the correct statement, which led to more conversations about details. Suddenly we all had renewed energy to tell the story now more completely! These newly found truthful details accelerated us.

My challenge to you is this: don't avoid continually seeking the moral to the story. The lessons learned are what shapes our reality. Don't discount the power of editing the story with newly found details if you believe they are true! When you need to make corrections, make the corrections; it won't weaken your (life) story, it will strengthen it!

The same is true of the stories we tell to ourselves in our daily lives. Humble reflection and commitment to seek truth is essential to re-write our stories and give us the fulfillment we crave.

We humans are very strange. We crave change and fear change at the same time. We love the repetition of rhythm in music but only so much. We love our favorite foods but will quickly hate them if we're forced to eat them every day. The idea of stretching out on the couch with a book can sound like heaven and then two hours after laying there we've gotta get up and move!

We're meant to live a dynamic life. We are meant to fly high on the winds of change. Our very health and vitality depend on it. We must boldly enter new chapters armed with new knowledge. We must take action in the moments we are given *while* continually checking our beliefs and refining our knowledge.

Gleaning the morals and defining principles from our stories is not meant to be a one-and-done process, but rather a continual flow that helps us catch the wind as we fly around the story flywheel.

EXERCISE: What is the Moral?

Following the prompts under Step 6, fill in the morals to your stories. Continue your daily stories, paying attention to resistance, authentic insights, the "why's", etc.

STEP SEVEN: ADVANCE

Story creates energy. This final step in the telling phase is all about applying that energy in the most effective way in order to accelerate and **advance**. As we think about this final step in the cycle of Story Acceleration, let's review what we've come through in the second phase.

We have framed the process with an extreme dedication to authenticity. We have reflected and determined the lessons learned. We hold onto them loosely enough to reassess when new data is available, but tightly enough to take action and apply new tactics.

Now we must plan *how* to tell our story. The most effective storytelling doesn't happen by accident. There is an optimal time, audience, and place for every story.

To leverage your stories most effectively the following questions must be answered in order to advance:

1. Who needs to hear this?
2. Where will it be told?
3. When will it be told?
4. What format / style will be most effective (video, written, in person)?

This final step in Story Acceleration has a very practical and tactical process that can be fun and energizing, but we must also be very intentional to execute the telling *complete with* describing the new plan based on the lessons learned.

By finishing our stories with a declaration about our future (e.g., how we'll apply what we've learned), we're going back into the writing phase and shepherding the story toward the goals we aim to achieve.

It's frightening how often humans give up *right before* the final stages of breakthrough. It's as if the forces that oppose us rally all their strength in a final surge as we fight the battle to complete.

To be honest, I feel that resistance right now as I near the end of writing this book. I am struggling to organize, find the energy, push myself to get up early and keep writing. This fatigue is a sign that we're close! It signals the importance to keep fighting and achieve the breakthrough.

Because this final step, the act of telling our stories and applying what we've learned is so vital and there is often so much resistance, I find it helpful to stop and reframe the situation. Seeing opportunity from a prisoner's point of view can give us the final burst of energy needed to execute on telling our story.

I've never been to jail or prison so I can't pretend to understand the experience deeply. I've only had two small experiences which help me imagine how hard it must be. I was detained by an officer once as a teenager. She placed me in the back of her cruiser and administered a series of field sobriety tests. It was only ten minutes or so before she confirmed I was sober and let me go on my way, but it felt like hours.

Later as an adult, when flying into Vancouver, Canadian border patrol decided I seemed suspicious and detained me in a locked waiting room for a few hours to make me sweat. It felt like days. I was innocent, but the longer I sat there with time to think the more frustrated I became, which probably made me seem more suspicious. When they did finally release me, the feeling of freedom brought an almost surreal level of elation.

Still these couple experiences are nothing like an extended loss of freedom or long-term challenge. I imagine the phrase: "When I get out...." must be a very common thought among inmates in prison.

Think about it for a moment. Imagine if you really did screw up and went to prison for a time. Wouldn't you just dream of all the possibilities and long for the opportunity to make progress toward a better life despite the challenges?

In prison, the challenges of "normal life" must seem easy, even silly, to someone doing time.

Freedom is the most valuable thing we have. The freedom to keep learning and taking steps forward by trying new ideas and applying what we learn.

Yet freedom is so common for most of us, we take it for granted to the point of boredom, living with little intent, just waiting for something to happen!

This habit can also be a prison if we refuse to move forward.

Compared to floating along with lack of intention, there is a much more serious prison we all must break out of in order to advance our story, and that is our own beliefs about our value and the importance of our story.

Prison Break - Part 1 (The Prequel)

It kills me to remember his face. It showed the perfect balance of approval and sadness.

"I think it will be better if I go, Dad. I've loved working here with you these last 6 years, but... I'm becoming more of a filmmaker than a marketer. I think I can get really good at it."

With a kind smile and slight nod my dad listened closely as I explained the opportunity I had: to write and direct a feature film.

In truth, I didn't love working that marketing job, I just loved being around my dad. My dad is the kindest man I've ever met, perhaps to a fault. Even though his business is a small company in which I could make a large impact, I didn't feel challenged, and I had slowly drifted over the years into a meaningless punch in, punch out oblivion.

As I said goodbye to my dad, I knew I would miss him, but I couldn't run fast enough from the windowless cubicles and sickly green fluorescent lights.

In almost no time, my house was sold, and I was in a truck heading toward Indiana with my wife and three kids. My younger brother and sister also moved with us. Together we were becoming professional filmmakers in a hurry. I had no idea what story I would create as a feature film, but I was sure determined to make it happen!

My older sister and brother-in-law had expressed excitement about working together and making an indie film. For some reason they believed in me and it meant the world to me.

While driving that big moving truck along toward Indiana, I kept thinking about the conversation with my dad. The look on his face. Then I imagined him watching my finished feature film. I imagined him saying how proud of me he is. I'm not kidding when I say I think I pressed the gas pedal a little harder.

When we arrived, we got straight to work. We rented and renovated a small production office and my brother and I started writing a story. The plan was to write the script in 3 months and go into pre-production as soon as possible. I had never written a feature. I didn't even know how to properly format it, but I hammered away at the outline together with my brother. He and I would take walks around the town discussing the potential storylines, characters, and plot while we walked.

When we got tired of walking, we'd go upstairs and throw a tennis ball back and forth in an empty dance studio, all while verbally processing our story.

We didn't have any money, but I didn't care! The sale of our house paid off more than $20K worth of credit card debt. We were essentially starting over. The budget for the film was so small it only paid for our apartment, so Bethany worked in the evening as a waitress. I would take over with the kids, get them fed, bathed, in bed. Then I went back to writing. I was coming alive.

Within 3 months, we somehow had a script. There it was: a movie spread over 120 pages. I could watch it in my mind, and I liked it! We had a plan, now we needed a team.

So I got to work reaching out and recruiting talented people through the internet. Each time the offer was similar: "We have little money to pay, but here's the script. We think it has shot. We'll cover your expenses, join us!"

Somehow people said yes. Everything was coming together. I could see it really happening! I realized I was made for this. I could feel myself growing every day. Revising the script, adding to our "mood board", finding locations, finding talent through casting sessions. We were gaining momentum, harnessing energy to lift us off the ground!

Then one night while I was editing my script my phone rang, I picked it up and heard my brother-in-law (our exec producer) on the other end:

"Jed, I need you to sit down."

His tone was shaky. His tone is never shaky.

It was the same exact phrase my dad had said to Becky, my older sister, when he called her to tell her about Jeremy's death so many years ago: "I need you to sit down."

My heart stopped. I sat down.

"Your dad had a major stroke today while receiving an award in Paris. He's in a coma. They're not sure if he'll pull through."

When you get news like that in a time of momentum, it's the most gut-wrenching, time-stopping punch in the face. Why him? Why now?

All we could do was pray for days on end and wait. Finally, a doctor let us know they were going to keep him in a coma in order to slow the bleeding in his brain. They informed us he would be under for a month.

I kept working. I would take time each day to pray as deeply as I could. Then without knowing what else to do, I kept preparing for the film production.

After a month, they brought him out of a coma. He couldn't walk or talk; they weren't sure if the blood vessels in his head would simply hemorrhage and stroke again. After another few weeks of lying in a bed in the French hospital and listening to nothing but French being spoken all around him and on the TV hanging above his bed, he said his first words... in

French. He didn't know French, but his brain was rewiring.

I met at my older sister and brother-in-law's house one night to discuss the next steps. After talking about dad, we turned the topic back to the film.

"I paid a professional screenwriter to read the script and give us notes," Mark said. "I want you to read what he sent me."

I proceeded to read pages and pages of scathing words such as "This is ridiculous" and "I don't even know what I am reading here" and "I can't get through this". The notes concluded with the statement (paraphrased): "I strongly recommend you *do not* make this film. It will be a giant waste of time."

I sat silently, pondering what to do. My head was swimming with excuses and defensive thoughts. I was frustrated. Finally, I looked up and said, "He is used to reading well formatted scripts that follow particular rules. But I wrote this not to be a book that people read, but as my own road map to make the film."

Mark thought about it for a while and the eternal optimist returned. After more discussion we decided to further edit the script and proceed with making the film.

They finally were able to fly my dad and my mom back to the states. Instead of returning to Syracuse where they lived, they came to us in Indiana.

The day I was finally able to see him again, I prepared myself to see a thin sickly man in a wheelchair. That didn't matter to me. He was alive and even if he couldn't remember me, I believed he would at some point.

When I entered the hospital room, his face lit up with recognition and he stretched open his one arm for a hug. Again, I came back to life.

Over the following months, we made our feature film, a psychological thriller called, *Silk Trees*.

Every day or so I would go visit my dad and dream of the day I'd be able to show him the art I had created with his other children. He would try to talk but couldn't say the most important part of the sentence. He'd say, "Do... you... think... we... can..." but couldn't say the final word. It was hard to watch him struggle, but we would share a tearful smile and hug when he'd simply give up and go back to saying the one thing he could always say clearly: "I love you."

As much as I wanted him to improve and watch my film, he never did. He spent the next 7 years struggling to get his brain back and after many more mini strokes, he finally passed away.

It wasn't until years later when I interviewed a Vietnam vet that I understood the impact this made on me. The vet was a marine and he described in vivid detail the agony of waiting for combat. After training so hard and living with deep expectations, to not realize those plans felt almost crippling, as if you can't move on until you finally do this one thing.

He himself did finally see combat but he explained that it was almost worse for his brothers who deployed and never fought. I'm not really trying to compare my situation to theirs. I imagine there must be nothing worse than experiencing war firsthand.

But I was in a type of mental prison.

We didn't know how to sell our feature film but even worse, I couldn't show my dad why I left his company. I couldn't make him proud of me. This haunted me. After the film was finished, we moved to Massachusetts, and I attempted to get a couple more films off the ground. I thought I would simply progress from directing one film project to the next. But it didn't work out that way.

It took a few years to finally get past a mini identity crisis. I found it difficult to shake a recurring thought: *I'm a filmmaker who is failing to make films.*

I knew I had many skills but that didn't feel important to me anymore because I wasn't doing what I wanted to do: direct movies every day.

One night, right around the time of that breakthrough I wrote about in the beginning of this book (when my electricity was cut), I was laying in the bathtub thinking: *What kind of filmmaker doesn't make films?*

No sooner had I thought this when I heard a calm, kind voice say in reply, "You're more than a filmmaker. You're an entrepreneur."

That's what it took for my identity to finally shift. I suddenly felt the importance of growing as an entrepreneur. I suddenly saw that I had been cutting my identity short of its fullest potential. Making films was only one thing out of many I could do and become good at.

After that, I truly leaned into the process of learning business in the real world and building a film production company, one daily story at a time.

My prison break wasn't from the corporate job where I worked with my father. My prison break was really seven years of building a new identity by trying ideas, battling through conflicts, staring at the ceiling in reflection each night, and applying what I learned when I woke up the next morning.

The Story of You

Your life is a never-ending series of episodes. People are watching. Who will you become? What will you achieve? What is standing in your way?

Our brains have experienced the pain and pleasure cycle since the day we were born. Yet the fear of pain often outweighs the hope for pleasure.

Why?

Because we have thousands of personal stories being embedded into our psyche from the day we are born. Stories with happy and sad endings, truthful and untruthful maxims, accurate and inaccurate lessons learned. The stories which were never accurately processed add up into a jumbled web, clouding our vision like a veil.

But Story Acceleration, an intentional journey around the story flywheel, by its nature *records* the lessons you've learned, reduces fear, and arms you with wisdom, courage, and energy, no matter story time horizon.

Over time, we can and do change. Think about the friends and acquaintances you had in high school and or college. If you're in your 20s you can probably already see the interesting changes happening to people since high school. If you're older than 30 you can see the spectacular change in people! The nerd that went on to become a multi-millionaire, the shy and homely teenage girl who is now a stunning and confident woman, the once popular jock who now sells cars. Or how about that friend who slowly drifted into using heavy drugs?

Whatever your past has been, it does not determine your future. If you want to do more than sell cars, build an automotive empire, or change careers! If you want to leave the drugs behind, you can!

Everyone must make the choice of whether they will relentlessly pursue growth (and enjoy the benefits), or simply settle for the easier path. We don't get to choose this one time, but rather we must make this choice every day, forever!

The process of advancing your story isn't without challenges. It will be filled with conflict. It already has been. But on the other side of carefully processed conflict is a more meaningful life, and untold amounts of joy!

FINAL EXERCISE: Share

It's time to share the stories you have created with the world. Not all of these will be appropriate to share publicly, some may only be suited for you to tell verbally to your closest friends or perhaps your family. Some will be perfect for short blog articles or videos you can share. Use the workbook to fill out the final steps.

CONCLUSION

There is no holding back time. We can't go back and re-write any chapter, though we might want to. Every single day matters. By the end of your life, the collection of stories you've written will amount to something. Will it be an epic tale of adventure, growth, and love? Or will it be a tragedy filled mostly with regrets because of debilitating insecurity or paralyzing fear?

It's 100% up to you.

Run into battle... run toward the conflict and fight! The fight is not against other people; the fight is inside of you!

Fight laziness.

Fight the fear of failure.

Fight the temptation to quit.

Fight the temptation to accept the status quo!

Fight against the foggy haze of wandering aimless through your story.

Fight against the lie that says only money and shiny things are what determine your value and joy.

Fight against the ego that comes from "success", but instead be humble and give away untold amounts of love!

By choosing to improve every step of Story Acceleration, especially in the daily bite sized stories you are writing, you will dramatically improve your life and the lives of those around you!

Be patient and keep going.

Keep writing and telling more truthful, authentic, and powerful stories... first to yourself, then to the world!

APPENDIX

Step One: Visualize Achievement

1. Dr Sanjay Gupta, "To 'Keep Sharp' This Year, Keep Learning, Advises Neurosurgeon Sanjay Gupta," interview by Terry Gross, *Fresh Air*, NPR, January 4, 2021, audio, https://www.npr.org/sections/health-shots/2021/01/04/953188905/to-keep-sharp-this-year-keep-learning-advises-neurosurgeon-sanjay-gupta

2. John Bryant, *3:59.4: The Quest for the Four-Minute Mile* (London: Hutchinson, 2004)

3. Ecc. 1:9 KJV

4. Karl Pillemer, PhD, *30 Lessons for Living: Tried and True Advice from the Wisest Americans* (New York: Penguin Group, 2011)

Step Two: Take Action

1. Napoleaon Hill, *Think and Grow Rich* (Meriden: The Ralston Society, 1937)
2. Stephen Pressfield, *The War of Art* (New York: Rugged Land, 2002), 158
3. Stephen Pressfield, *The War of Art* (New York: Rugged Land, 2002), 51
4. Stephen Covey, *7 Habits of Highly Effective People*, (New York: Free Press, 1989)
5. *The Simpsons*, episode 6, "The Cartridge Family," created by Matt Groening, November 2, 1997, on Fox Network.

Step Three: Navigate Conflict

1. Anna Spafford, "Family Tragedy," Library of Congress, April 29, 2021, https://www.loc.gov/exhibits/americancolony/amcolony-family.html
2. Viktor Frankl, *Man's Search for Meaning: An Introduction to Logotherapy*, (Boston: Beacon Press 1959), 81.
3. Viktor Frankl, *Man's Search for Meaning: An Introduction to Logotherapy*, (Boston: Beacon Press 1959), 82.

4. Viktor Frankl, *Man's Search for Meaning: An Introduction to Logotherapy*, (Boston: Beacon Press 1959), 82.

5. National Foundation for American Policy, *Immigrants and Billion Dollar Startups*, by Stuart Anderson, 2016.

Step Four: Develop Character

1. "Footage Shows Homeless Man Giving His Life to Save a Female Hostage from A Gunman," *FOX 29 Philadelphia*, September 10, 2015, https://www.fox29.com/news/footage-shows-homeless-man-giving-his-life-to-save-a-female-hostage-from-a-gunman

2. Donald Miller, *Building a Story Brand*, (New York: HarperCollins Leadership, 2017)

3. *Star Wars: Episode IV - Return of the Jedi*, directed by Richard Marquand. (1983; Los Angeles, CA: 200th Century Studios, Inc.)

4. *Les Miserables*, directed by Billy August (1998; United Kingdom, Columbia Pictures)

5. "'Handcuffs to Handshakes': A journey of forgiveness and friendship," *FOX61*, https://www.fox61.com/article/news/local/mi

chigan-life/handcuff-to-handshakes-bad-cop-victim-reconnect/69-191467ba-8bd3-4bbc-bc17-5a4fd04e766e

6. Caroline Torie, "Convicted: Two Benton Harbour men tell their story," *WSBT22*, Sept. 19, 2017, https://wsbt.com/news/local/convicted-two-benton-harbor-men-tell-their-story

7. Caroline Torie, "Convicted: Two Benton Harbour men tell their story," *WSBT22*, Sept. 19, 2017, https://wsbt.com/news/local/convicted-two-benton-harbor-men-tell-their-story

8. Joel Porter, "Former cop and wrongly convicted man share story of forgiveness," *WNDU*, Geb. 25, 2016, https://www.wndu.com/content/news/Former-cop-and-wrongly-convicted-man-share-story-of-forgiveness-370215411.html?clmob=y

9. Joel Porter, "Former cop and wrongly convicted man share story of forgiveness," *WNDU*, Geb. 25, 2016, https://www.wndu.com/content/news/Former

-cop-and-wrongly-convicted-man-share-story-of-forgiveness-370215411.html?clmob=y

10. Steve Hartman, "Innocent Man Ends Up Pals With Crooked Cop That Framed Him," *CBS*, April 17, 2016, https://www.kcentv.com/article/life/innocent-man-ends-up-pals-with-crooked-cop-that-framed-him/83-138666008

11. https://www.kcentv.com/article/life/innocent-man-ends-up-pals-with-crooked-cop-that-framed-him/83-138666008

Step Five: Think Authentically

1. Zachary Crockett, "The Art Forger Who Became a National Hero," *Priceonomics,* *https://priceonomics.com/the-art-forger-who-became-a-national-hero/*

2. Zachary Crockett, "The Art Forger Who Became a National Hero," *Priceonomics,* *https://priceonomics.com/the-art-forger-who-became-a-national-hero/*

3. "Art: Truth & Consequences," *Time*, November 24, 1947,

http://content.time.com/time/subscriber/artic
le/0,33009,887772,00.html

4. *It's a Wonderful Life*, directed by Frank Capra.
(1946; Manhattan, NY: RKO Radio Pictures)

ABOUT THE AUTHOR

Jed Burdick is a filmmaker, entrepreneur and owner of Votary Films in Worcester, MA. He and his team are dedicated to telling meaningful stories and teaching others the value in their stories. He currently lives in New England with his wife, Bethany, their five sons and daughter.

Made in the USA
Middletown, DE
12 March 2022

62326645R00144